Letters to Darcy is not an acknowledgment of a short life—it is a celebration of an *eternal* life. Tenderly and honestly written, this look into a courageous woman's soul evokes tears and admiration for the parents who can adore a little girl and relinquish her to God with the certainty of absolute faith.

—ANGELA HUNT, AUTHOR OF *SHE'S IN A BETTER PLACE*

TRACY RAMOS

letters
to

*a mother's heartfelt letters
to her unborn child*

Tyndale House Publishers, Inc.
Carol Stream, Illinois

Library of Congress Cataloging-in-Publication Data

Ramos, Tracy.
    Letters to Darcy / Tracy Ramos.
        p. cm.
    ISBN 978-1-4143-3384-7 (hc)
1. Mother and infant—Miscellanea. 2. Mothers—Correspondence.
3. Letters. 4. Mother and child. 5. Pro-life movement—United States.
I. Title.
    HQ755.84.R35 2009
    306.874′3092—dc22   2009023246

Printed in the United States of America

15 14 13 12 11 10 09
 7   6   5   4   3   2   1

Acknowledgments

To God, for Your unconditional love;

To Jason, for making every second count;

To Brittany, Isabella, Alexys, Mallorie, Roman, and Bryson, for giving me the reason to keep going;

To Grace Community Church of Magnolia, for being Christ's hands and feet;

To our family and friends, for their love and support;

To thousands who have lifted us in prayer;

To our friends at Tyndale, for helping spread Darcy's message to the world;

And to my sweet Darcy, my inspiration,

Thank you.

Foreword

There comes a time in one's life when a single decision changes everything. For Tracy and Jason Ramos, that decision was to allow their unborn daughter Darcy Anne to live. Faced with the reality that she was carrying a baby with trisomy 18, Tracy was given the option of ending the pregnancy early, after being assured that her baby was not compatible with life. The Ramoses chose life over death because of their faith in a sovereign God who does all things for His glory. Darcy Anne arrived a few months later as a beautiful bundle of joy, just like the Ramoses' previous six children.

Although Darcy Anne's life expectancy was only a few hours, God kept her alive for fifteen amazing days to teach each of us some valuable lessons about life. This gift from God reminded us that life is measured not in days but in daily experiences. Tracy and Jason knew that because their time with Darcy Anne would be short, their memories would have to be long. And so, each hour of Darcy's life was filled with the joys that most girls have years to enjoy: birthday parties, hugs and kisses, painted toenails, and even a ride on her daddy's motorcycle. Tracy and Jason treasured each memory with Darcy Anne as if it would be the last.

You are about to read Tracy's thoughts that were

captured in her Web diary. Hundreds were reading about the daily emotions the Ramoses experienced. People who did not know Tracy and Jason began watching a fragile life change the world, one heart at a time. As it turns out, this little four-pound-seven-ounce bundle of joy provided an international audience with a message that should never be forgotten: *Each day we live should be for God's glory, and each of us brings glory to God by the way we live each day.*

Tracy and Jason chose life over death for their daughter, and she brought great glory to God as a missionary for life. Those of us who lived this journey with the Ramos family will be forever changed. For those of you who will read of this journey, my hope is that you will see how God has a plan for everything He creates. Darcy Anne is a testimony that life is precious from the moment of conception and that it is given to humankind to fulfill a purpose. Darcy Anne's purpose was to bring a family together, to unite a church, to remind all of us of how we are to live our lives, regardless of their length.

—Ted Seago
Honored pastor of Darcy Anne Ramos
Grace Community Church
Magnolia, Texas

february

Wednesday, February 6, 2008

This was one of the most beautiful days of my life. I just found out that I am pregnant. Even though we were not planning on having any more children, God had other plans. You are our first surprise baby, and I know that you are special because God has chosen for you to become part of our family. Inside, I was leaping with joy. I saw the plus sign on the pregnancy test, and joy filled my heart. I had felt a void from the decision we made to not have another baby. But God intervened and filled that void. I was overwhelmed with gladness.

Wednesday, February 13, 2008

I waited a week to tell your daddy because I knew he would be shocked. I actually first told your aunt Nekita and then your big sister Ate Brittany.[1] I wanted to explode with excitement and tell everyone, but for the first time in your mommy's life, I showed self-control.

Saturday, February 16, 2008

Today was our church's Valentine's Day party. We had a great time. I was mostly excited about telling everyone that I was pregnant with you. Darcy, our church really loves babies and got so excited to hear

---

[1] *Ate* (pronounced *ah-tee*) means "older sister" in the Philippines.

about you. They really were so happy. Daddy even sang me a special song. He forgot the words, but it was still really pretty. He sang "And I Love You So." Now whenever I hear that song, I will think of you.

Saturday, February 23, 2008

This was my first real scare. I started having crippling pains and bleeding. I just knew that I was going to lose you. I was devastated. I knew that I was given this seventh chance and now it was over. I gave up all hope.

Sunday, February 24, 2008

The bleeding continued all night. I decided to stay home from church and rest. The bleeding finally stopped at noon. I was so relieved. I was glad but still very anxious.

Monday, February 25, 2008:
First Sonogram

Today, I decided to go to the doctor and have an exam. I wasn't scheduled for my visit till next week, but since I was having problems, they went ahead and saw me. They did a sonogram and said everything looked good. I even got to see and hear your heartbeat. Never was I happier. You were a fighter from the very beginning, just like Mommy!

I love you, Darcy. I love you so much.

march

Saturday, March 1, 2008

Well, the bleeding started back up. It seems like this is happening again. It only lasts for about twelve hours and stops. This time isn't as bad as the last. It sure does scare Mommy when this happens. I hope you are okay.

Sunday, March 2, 2008

I decided to stay home again from church. I am very nervous about doing anything strenuous. I want to make sure you are okay.

Wednesday, March 5, 2008

Today was my first legitimate doctor's appointment. I got so sick that I threw up everywhere. Don't worry, Darcy. I think it was food poisoning and not morning sickness (even though I've had a lot of that, too). Dr. Ritter was very nice and did not make me endure the exam but rather just talked to me about what to expect and the extra tests I could get if I wanted them. I also had Daddy pull over along the side of the road on our way home to throw up some more. I was very sick.

Saturday, March 8, 2008

The bleeding started up again. This seems to be happening once a week, on Saturdays. Maybe it

is because I tend to do more on the weekends.
I hope that I am not overdoing it. I will try to be
more careful on weekends. I have continued to
have crippling pains, and they seem to be getting
worse. It affects my arms and legs. I love you. I
have a doctor's appointment on Wednesday. I will
ask him what is going on then.

I love you and hope you are all right.

Sunday, March 9, 2008

I missed church two Sundays in a row and thought
I would go today. I talked to some ladies at church
about my symptoms and asked if they could be a
sign that something is wrong. But they gave me
some advice, and I am going to take it. When I got
home, my symptoms got really bad. I got a rash all
over my belly, and it itched so much. I am going
to my regular doctor tomorrow to see what he
says. I hope this is not a result of something being
wrong with you. I will pray.

Monday, March 10, 2008

I went to my doctor to see what is wrong with
me. He didn't want to diagnose me and referred me
back to my ob-gyn. I guess I will see what he wants
me to do.

Thursday, March 13, 2008

Remember when Mommy said that I was a fighter?
Well, I am stubborn, too. I waited till today to go
see Dr. Ritter. The pain is too bad to endure anymore. So I went after I had lunch with Daddy.

Dr. Ritter prescribed some steroids, and I need to take them. He didn't want to refer me to an allergist yet, just in case my symptoms cleared up. He did say that it has nothing to do with you and that you are not experiencing any bad side effects from the steroids or my symptoms.

Friday, March 14, 2008

Dr. Ritter has cured me. Steroids took all of my symptoms away. I must have been allergic to something. I've stopped eating all weird stuff. I hope I stay well and you are okay.

I love you, Darcy.

Wednesday, March 19, 2008

All of my symptoms have come back with a vengeance. I went back to Dr. Ritter. He is sending me to an allergist. I went to see her, and she gave me more steroids. She said to be careful with them because of the risk of getting gestational diabetes and having a big baby. She also referred me to a rheumatologist. The allergist wants me to make the earliest appointment with the rheumatologist, which is the middle of April. She ordered some blood tests. I will go tomorrow to have blood drawn.

Thursday, March 20, 2008

I went to have my blood drawn. Daddy and I have our regular lunch date since it is Thursday.

Sunday, March 23, 2008

It is Easter! And Bella gets to share Easter with
her birthday. We were going to go to Incredible
Pizza, but they were closed. We took her to CiCi's
instead. We will have to go to Incredible Pizza
some other time. Isabella's little secret sis made a
special cake for her. It was so pretty and yummy!

april

Wednesday, April 23, 2008

This is the day of my amniocentesis. I am really nervous. I have never had one before, but since I was having these issues, I wanted to make sure you were okay. I really am not too concerned. I know that you are all right.

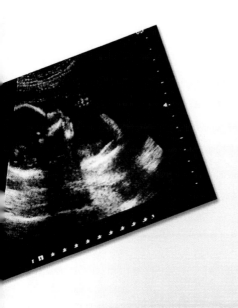

may

Thursday, May 1, 2008

My world came crashing down when I heard the
words *not compatible with life*. I was thinking,
What does that mean? I had just come home from a
wonderful lunch with Daddy, and Dr. Ritter called.
I didn't want to break down in front of the girls,
but soon I could hold back the tears no longer.
I finally got off the phone and called Daddy. He
didn't quite understand what I was saying because
I was crying so hard, but he understood that he
needed to come home quick.

Friday, May 2, 2008

Today is my birthday. I wouldn't say it's a happy
one. We started off the day talking to Dr. Ritter.
Daddy came with me, and for the first time he
really understood what we are up against. He
broke down. We are quickly becoming experts
on trisomy 18. I just feel awful. Your wonderful
sisters and brothers had this beautiful day planned,
and all I want to do is curl up and die.

Why did this have to happen to us? We have
never had anything really awful happen to us.
It was finally starting to set in what Daddy had
always said to me, that God has this hedge around
us and that He was setting us aside for something

special. Daddy always told me not to worry because of this hedge.

Tuesday, May 6, 2008: Amnio Results Confirmed

We are taking this one day at a time. Brittany is having a very hard time, as she is helping me with preparations. Buying things is especially hard because we know that we will not have Darcy long, if at all. Lexy broke down and cried through all of the church service on Sunday. She was inconsolable. It is just very hard. We are put in a situation in which we have to make a lifetime of memories in a short amount of time, and we don't want to have any regrets.

I want to thank everyone once again for their prayers.

Tuesday, May 6, 2008: The Ultrasound

The ultrasound specialist confirmed the results of the amniocentesis. Darcy has trisomy 18. We were still holding out hope that there was some kind of mistake and that she was going to be fine. But that was not to be. She currently has cysts on her brain and a hole that runs through all four chambers of her heart. In addition, she has rocker-bottom feet and clenched fists (these are only "minor" outward physical abnormalities, for which I am so thankful). She is a beautifully formed baby. Most of the damage is internal. Her kidneys, liver, and other organs look okay right now. We asked the doctor about her heart and possibly doing surgery (because this is the biggest concern right now). He said the heart, in and of itself, is the most serious issue but is not fatal. They will not elect to do surgery on her to repair it since she has a fatal disease, even though they would do surgery (for the same heart defect) on an otherwise healthy baby. I just don't understand it. Her chances of making it to term are fifty-fifty. At birth, they will only do comfort care. No lifesaving care will be administered.

Wednesday, May 7, 2008

Dear sweet Darcy,

I felt you move inside my belly for the very first time. I have been waiting for a while now. You are my miracle. My chosen gift from God. You are so special that God wants you back soon, but not before I get to feel your presence. I hope I get to meet you face-to-face so that you can see your mommy that God chose for you.

I also want you to see the blanket that Mommy started to make for you tonight. I hope you like it. I am really not that talented, but I am trying really hard to make it perfect. No matter what happens, Mommy will be with you. Jesus will protect you, and He will take you to a much better place than what you would have here with me. I thank Jesus Christ, my Lord and Savior, for choosing me to be the one to carry such a special blessing as you. He could have chosen anyone, but He wanted me to be a part of your life. Why He would choose me for such a perfect and special gift, I will never know. I am truly not worthy. I miss you terribly already. I hope God gives me the strength to endure. I can't even breathe. I can't wait to see your precious face.

Love,
Mommy

Thursday, May 8, 2008

Today I made you another bracelet. I am still working on your blanket. I will try to get Daddy to post some pictures of it later. He is very busy, and I don't know how to upload pictures. Darcy, there are a lot of people praying for you. Even in other parts of the world—the UK, India, Philippines, Dubai, Hungary—and here in the United States. Your aunt Dianne called and told me that she is a grandma today. Her granddaughter was due on my birthday but came a little late. Aunt Dianne was so happy that she couldn't wait to call. She called at 11:20 p.m. You don't even know it, but you have already made a difference in so many lives.

I love you.
Mommy

Friday, May 9, 2008

Darcy,

I can't seem to find the words to say. I like writing because it makes me feel close to you. I have been feeling down lately, so Ate Brittany gave me part of my Mother's Day gift early. And did she ever make me feel better. She made me a beautiful bracelet that has your name on it. I rewrapped it because I want to reopen it on Sunday and wear it to church. We were trying to find the perfect bracelet online so that we could have your name put on it. We found it, but instead of our paying the $118, Brittany made it instead, and it came out exactly the same. I love it and will cherish it always.

Love,
Mommy

Saturday, May 10, 2008

Hi, Darcy.

Tomorrow is Mother's Day. I am going to celebrate it with you, as it may be the only Mother's Day that I will have you with me, alive and kicking. I will try to smile and be happy for God giving me this day with you. You are my gift for Mother's Day. You would truly be amazed at all the love and support that are given to your mommy and daddy just because of you, and not just from family and friends. Even people I have never met have given of themselves. How do you thank people for this? Words are just not enough. I hope that if not in this life, maybe in the life to come I can be blessed by their presence so that I can share with them how God has blessed me through their kindness. God is good, Darcy. God is so good!

Sunday, May 11, 2008

Today I woke up to breakfast in bed. You have the best siblings anyone could ever hope for. They pray for you every day. We then went to church. It was a good day. All of the daddies got up and sang to us in celebration of Mother's Day. They were all praising God, and they sounded great! After church we came home, and Daddy and I took a nap. When we woke up, we had dinner, and then we went out and Daddy bought me a ring that says, "Always and Forever." I thought it was a perfect gift, and I will always wear it to show that I will always and forever love you. When we came home, your sisters cleaned the whole house. I had a great day.

Tuesday, May 13, 2008

Today I went and set up your memorial fund at the bank. I'm looking forward to putting the fund to good use in your memory. How happy that would make me, that you would bring such joy and happiness to others!

I didn't write yesterday, but it wasn't because I didn't think about you. Your Ate Brittany and Mommy found the perfect headband for you. The ones we had bought previously just were not perfect enough for you. We're still searching for the perfect outfit. Mommy wants to make sure things are perfect before meeting you. I think you will like them. I can't wait to put them on you.

I am going to bed now.

I love you, Darcy.
Mommy

Thursday, May 15, 2008

Hi, Darcy.

Mommy found the perfect outfit at Sears! The lady checking me out kept saying how pretty it was. I started to cry and told her why. God brought her to me today, Darcy. She kept hugging and comforting me.

I see beautiful babies all around me. Kim, a sweet lady from church, had her baby today. I am so happy for her. I so wish that I could bring you home with me. That is my desire. I need you—your smell, your soft baby skin. I want to hold you so badly.

It seems so unnatural to plan, deliver, and hold you and then not be able to keep you. But God has other plans. I don't know how to deliver you and not bring you home. How do I sign a birth certificate and a death certificate so close together? How do I plan a birth and a funeral at the same time? It is just so unnatural.

I have to admit something to you, Darcy. Amid all of the confusion, I have never been closer to God than I am right now. He is holding you close to Him, and He is drawing *me* close to Him too. I know that when I can't seem to figure things out, He will show me the way, and He will direct my path. This is not the path I chose, but it is the path that glorifies Him. Praise God!

I love you, Darcy.
Mommy

Sunday, May 18, 2008

Dear Darcy,

Today was a beautiful day at church. We dedicated you and your brothers to the Lord, together with other parents and their children. The purpose of the dedication was to vow before God and each other to raise you and your brothers in the ways of Christ. The whole church vowed to help us do just that by keeping us accountable and helping wherever necessary in raising you and your siblings according to the principles of the Bible. I am so glad that I dedicated you to the One, the Most High, to protect you and trust Him in all of your life, no matter how long or short.

I also met a friend today through the Internet. God has been so gracious in sending people to comfort me. He is the Great Comforter, Darcy.

My friend's name is Becky. She owns a jewelry business in Houston and offered to make you and Mommy matching bracelets. She has been very reassuring. She is going to visit her niece, who is one month old. She told me that her niece was also diagnosed with a genetic abnormality (Down syndrome). But guess what? She came out perfectly normal! How is that for God's miracle?

Your daddy and I had a date at our favorite Greek restaurant. We talked about you and about how blessed we are to have you. We met some old friends we went to Crossroads with a few years ago, and we shared your story. They, too, will be praying. In fact, they may visit you at this site and drop a note very soon.

I love you very much.
Mommy

Monday, May 19, 2008

Dear Darcy,

Words cannot express my feelings now. Heavenly Angels in Need donated a beautiful gown. Cheryl, one of the volunteers, sewed the gown, bonnet, and quilt for you. My heart is just broken that people who don't even know me would donate their time, their wedding dresses, and money for mommies like me who have terminally ill babies. How could someone like me ever repay their generosity? This is a perfect example of finding joy while in the valley.

Darcy, Mommy is weak. I am very weak, even though people keep saying that I am strong. I can only drink of this cup because God is providing for my every need. God keeps sending people to me to love and comfort me until my cup over-flows. Darcy, I just can't explain why I am not mad at God. Everyone who knows me would tell you that my first reaction, regarding my children, is fierce and that I would fight to the death to pro-tect them. But God has given me the understand-ing that you are His, and I just feel like He wanted to bless me through your life—your life inside of me. And He wants to bless you by not leaving you here to suffer, not just suffer from your physical ailments but also from the things of this world. And, Darcy, I cannot even begin to tell you how many people He has blessed because of you. That makes you special. That makes you *very* special. And I love you so much. Love just doesn't seem like the right word for what I feel for you. I can't wait to see how beautiful God has made you.

I love you, sweetie.
Mommy

Wednesday, May 21, 2008

Hi, Darcy.
We made it to our first goal! I have been praying, and God has answered my prayer. Praise God! I am at twenty weeks! Yea! You are a strong baby, and I am so glad that you are still with me. Our next goal is to make it to twenty-five weeks. Mommy will be with you every second.

You made all the delicate, inner parts of my body and knit me together in my mother's womb. Thank you for making me so wonderfully complex! Your workmanship is marvelous—how well I know it.
PSALM 139:13-14

I went to Dr. Ritter's today for my ob-gyn appointment. After two Dopplers and problems with the second one, they found your little heartbeat. I was never so happy to hear it. It sounds very strong. Dr. Ritter told me that I can come in at any time throughout this pregnancy. He says I have a VIP ticket for sono-grams, appointments, or whatever else that I want.

He is a great doctor, and I am so happy that God led me to him. He wants me to monitor my blood sugar, because he doesn't want you to get too big. I guess, subconsciously—since I know that babies with your condition are usually small—I have been eating a lot so that you will be chunky. I know that it doesn't work that way and that my excess weight will only affect me, but I am going to try anyway.

I hope you are comfy and snug inside Mommy. I want you to feel safe, happy, and loved.

I love you.
Mommy

Thursday, May 22, 2008

Hi, Darcy.

This is a poem that a new and beautiful friend wrote for you. Her name is Mary Cate. She has been my closest friend, and God has helped me so much through her. She read your story and fol-lowed God's leading to e-mail Mommy, and she was so inspired by you that she wrote this poem. I hope you like it. Here it is. I love you, Darcy.

Thank You for Loving Me

Mommy and Daddy, I want you to know
I love you so.
I know you are scared and cry a lot.
Just know my love for you will never stop.
Thank you for loving me
And enjoying me as part of our awesome family.
I love living beneath your heart, Mommy, my dear,

While listening to my Daddy sing pretty songs.
My brothers and sisters are so neat.
I love you all.
You are very sweet.
I enjoy hearing you laugh, giggle, and run.
Today can be so much fun.
Just try to enjoy every day,
Don't focus on me going away.
I am right here with you now.
Jesus will give our family the grace
to get through the fear.
He is near.
Just lean on Him,
We have faith, hope, and love.
I already feel more love than some
kids do in a lifetime.
Thank you for loving me,
I am as happy as can be.

Friday, May 23, 2008

Dearest Darcy Anne,

I was struck with a ton of bricks tonight. I was
unable to sleep as a result. Remember when I told
you about my friend Mary Cate? Well, she sent
me the most comforting e-mail tonight, and I was
so overwhelmed by something she said that I had
to tell you. She said, "I sat here and cried earlier.
I don't want you to go through this. I told God
I would be willing to give my life for Darcy's; I
would trade her places if you could just keep her
with you."

Darcy, I keep asking myself, *How could someone who was but a stranger three days ago offer to give her life for yours?* And I thought about something Jesus said in John 15:13: "There is no greater love than to lay down one's life for one's friends."

I realized that Jesus wanted me to talk to you about Him. Jesus will overwhelm you with His presence when He calls you to be with Him. At that moment, He is going to give you another body that is perfect and without any affliction. Jesus chose you to be His child. And He is not one who is unfamiliar with pain and suffering. In fact, He suffered the most horrendous pain that there is, just so you could be with Him. His pain had a purpose, your pain has a purpose, and my pain has a purpose. I know that the pain that we experience is not for bad, but rather to mold us into who we are to be, according to His purpose. We have seen evidence of how He has molded you to help so many already. I believe that through your pain He will bring many to Himself. He is the great I Am! He is the Lion of Judah! He is the Comforter! He is the Savior of the world!

Romans 8:28 says, "We know that God causes everything to work together for the good of those who love God and are called according to his purpose for them."

Oh, the joy that awaits you and those who are called.

You are so loved. Oh, how I love you. But God loves you more, sweetie!

Thank You, Lord, for blessing me with this beautiful child.

Love,
Mommy

Saturday, May 24, 2008

Dear Darcy,

I want to share with you a story about something that happened today. I had a mommy-daughter date with your three older sisters. We went to see a movie and then went to Bennigan's to have lunch. When we had finished eating and asked for the check, the waitress came over and said that the table next to us had paid our bill. They told her that they wanted to bless us today. They left before I knew of their generosity. It is just another way that God is leading people, strangers we don't even know, to bless us. They did not know about you, but God is doing beautiful things for me to help me feel better. You are going to be with God, and this is a tiny example of how He knows our needs and provides.

Here is a song that your older sister Alexys wrote for you. It talks about her faith in God.

I'll Have Some Faith in You

In any thing you do, I'll have some faith in you.
And even if you don't heal her,
I still will understand.
But, if you do heal her, I'll be glad you did.
In any thing you do, I'll have some faith in you.

And either way you choose, I'll have some faith in you.
  Either way you choose, I'll have some faith in you.

—Alexys Brooke Ramos, 2008

Sunday, May 25, 2008

Dear Darcy,
I love you.
Mommy

Monday, May 26, 2008

Dear Darcy,
Today is Memorial Day! We all went to Splash-town today. Your siblings loved going down the big waterslides. As I was lying in the kiddie pool, watching your brothers, I was hoping you were relaxing as the water rushed over my belly.

I have been a little down lately. It is hard for Mommy to find complete joy in things that I used to do. It is very hard.
I love you very much.
Mommy

Wednesday, May 28, 2008

I had a dream about you today. You were the most perfectly formed baby, without any illness. The doctors were amazed that nothing was wrong with you. You lived and had a normal, healthy child-hood. If only that were a sign of things to come. What a testimony that would be of God's mercy and grace. However, if not in this life, definitely in the life to come. I can always be comforted by the fact that you will be free of ailment with Jesus as you serve and praise Him on the streets of gold. God is merciful for giving me this dream to be a constant reminder of how I want to always remember you, even if only in heaven.

I pray for you, as others are.

I love you very much.
Mommy

Thursday, May 29, 2008

Good morning, Darcy.

Something happened today that really touched me. As I was leaving for my typical lunch date with Daddy, I noticed the lawn was mowed. I called Daddy to see if he did it, and much to my surprise, he said no. Somebody else mowed our grass. After calling around, I found out who. It was Angela, our neighbor across the street! She wrote on your blog. Can you believe that? She realized that Daddy was running behind in his lawn duties because he was trying to help Mommy the best he could to deal with this . . . and it's really hot outside! This is just another example of God working through His people to help us in our time of need. What a great God we serve! Darcy, you will know what I mean when you meet Him face-to-face.

Angela has also helped Mommy with your big sister Mallie. She takes her to the park and invites her to dinner. I guess Mommy hasn't felt like doing much lately, and she wants to help Mommy by taking Mallie with her when she takes her little girl and boy, Lexy and Jake. She and our other neighbors keep asking how they can help, but I am not one to ask, and neither is Daddy. I guess God is laying on people's hearts the best way to help, and then they do. We really couldn't do this without the prayers, love, and support that we are getting from people around the world.

Mommy and Daddy love you so much, Darcy. As do so many others. . . .

Mommy

Thursday, June 5, 2008

Dear Darcy,

I was so moved today. I went to see your daddy lead his Bible study, and he was spectacular. He has been leading it for a while, but today was the first time that I went. I was so blessed by the way the Holy Spirit moved. I pray that somehow the Lord relayed the message to you. I am sure that you recognized Daddy's voice. He is definitely blessed to teach God's word. I almost decided to start keeping my journal to you private. I have talked to Daddy for a few days about not keeping it public. Daddy wanted me to pray about it to make sure that it is what the Lord wants because he felt like I should keep it public. And wouldn't you know it, God answered my prayer yesterday when I received an e-mail from a lady from our church, Sherree. I am convinced now, that He wants me to continue keeping this journal to you public. He amazes me how he answers our prayers through His people. She really blessed me yesterday with her prayers and words of encouragement. This along with a story that Daddy told me was evidence that I should continue to share my thoughts, about you, to everyone. He works with a lady who has two children and told him that she would have an abortion if she got pregnant again. Then, just a few weeks ago, she told him after reading about you, she wouldn't dream of doing it. If for only that, I am glad that God led us to do this Web site.

Like I said, Darcy, God is blessing so many people just by your story.

I love you so much,

Mommy

june

Monday, June 2, 2008

My precious Darcy,

I wonder how you are doing. I wonder if you are growing and comfortable. I wonder if you know how much you are truly loved. I hope that Jesus helps you realize, like only He can, all of the love that surrounds you.

You know, Darcy, when mommies and daddies go through trials like these, Satan will attack from all different angles. He has been on the prowl, but he is not the victor. God is victorious. The God who loves you, Darcy, is the same God who loves Mommy and Daddy. God will not be mocked, and He will not let the devil reign in the lives of those who belong to Jesus.

Darcy, when you go to be with Jesus, ask about your brothers or sisters that God has already called. They will be there to greet you too, and you will have fun playing with them as y'all are praising Jesus and waiting for Mommy and Daddy and your other brothers and sisters. You will also be greeted by friends, like Catelyn,[2] and other family members, like Meema[3] and Lolo.[4] Be sure to tell Meema that Mommy had two boys. She will not

---

[2] Catelyn was a friend's baby who died in the womb.
[3] Nickname for Grandma
[4] Philippine nickname for Grandpa

believe it. Also, tell her that you are number seven. She won't believe that either. Tell her one more thing. Tell her that I named you after her because she meant so much to me while she was here and that I love her so much and still think about her often. You are going to be so loved in heaven, like you are here on earth. You will be surrounded by many friends and family there, like you would be here.

I love you very much and always will.
Mommy

Wednesday, June 4, 2008

Dear Darcy,

Mommy has been really down lately. The last two weeks have been really hard on Mommy. I really don't want to lose you. I want you to stay here with me. I have really been having bad feelings toward those people who didn't want me to have you. I am struggling a lot. How could they not want me to have you? Now since you will be leaving me, I really resent it.

I have not been wanting to do anything. My life is just in shambles. I haven't been going to church or wanting to be around people. I haven't wanted to clean, cook, or anything. Your daddy left me two weeks ago because he couldn't stand the mess anymore. How could he leave me and stay out all night? Especially now, when I am having to go through losing you, and especially over something as minor as a mess. He has never done that before.

Not in nineteen years. I just feel all alone. I really feel alone and hurt. I feel as if I have to go through this alone. I feel as if to please your siblings, I can't get on them for not doing their chores or picking up after themselves. But to please Daddy, I have to scream at them all day to not leave their stuff out. One person will leave if I don't scream, and others are emotionally hurt if I do scream. And I don't even want to deal with them. I want to be with you. I don't know how much more I can take.

I don't mean for this to be dark. I want to help others through your life now. God is helping others through your story. I don't want to let you down or let God down, or my family down, or friends, but it seems as if that is all I am doing. I feel like I have to be strong for everyone. Everyone is watching me. How will I handle things? Well, Darcy, Mommy is weak. I can't be strong anymore. Daddy doesn't want to be here. The kids don't want to be here. Even *I* don't want to be here. Maybe God will take me, too, when He takes you, so you won't be alone, and I won't be alone. I feel useless to people now. God doesn't need me here to mess up everyone's life. Maybe your Lola was right. Maybe with you Brittany does have one more sibling to raise and I am useless.

I don't even know how to end such a horrible entry. Maybe I will delete it later.

I love you.
Mommy

Thursday, June 5, 2008

Dear Darcy,

Last night, I could feel the raining down of prayers being said for you and your family. Thank you to Mary Cate, my prayer warrior and your adoptive aunt. You will never know what your support means to me.

Last night when Daddy read my post, he came to me and told me that he had read it. I could tell by the look in his eyes that he realized the level of hurt that was caused by his leaving. He vowed that he would never leave his family again. I think for the first time in a long time he heard me and felt my pain. He was so compassionate and loving and really wanted to make things right. He is a very godly man and one focused on doing the right thing, especially when it comes to his family. I want to quote Daddy on something: "I just want you to know that I love you. I never mean to hurt you. I wish I could rewind every time I hurt you." What a wonderful thing to say. I can't wait for you to meet him and see how wonderful he is.

Darcy, sometimes when families go through something like this, it breaks them apart, something Satan would love to see happen. But sometimes it makes them stronger. That is what is happening now. God showed us mercy and gave us the grace of healing. Daddy and I contemplated taking out the last entry, but we decided to leave it as evidence of the bumpy road that we are encountering and as evidence of what is making us stronger.

This is a bittersweet journey—sweet in that we are getting closer to meeting you, my most precious baby. And on the flip side, we are one day closer to giving you back to Jesus.

Darcy, I pray that my stress is not causing you undue stress. I know it is, but I hope you hang in there with Mommy.

I love you, sweet Darcy.
Mommy

Monday, June 9, 2008
Dear Darcy,

Pastor Mark preached yesterday, and one of the things that he said helped me. He spoke about faith and about walking in faith and not by sight. It reminded me of Hebrews 11:1: "Faith is the confidence that what we hope for will actually happen; it gives us assurance about things we cannot see." This is such a wonderful verse to remember when dealing with troubling things. If we rely on what we see, we see evidence of a grim prognosis that leads to death. But faith is walking the path that God sets before us without knowing what the future holds. He could be setting us up for the path of life. And there have been so many evidences of life that we have witnessed because of your story.

I must share a story about a sweet lady at church who brings me so much comfort. Her name is Colleen. The first day I went back to church after finding out about you, she came up and gave me a hug and didn't say one word. It was, and still is, so hard to talk about, and she was so sweet to not say anything. Sometimes actions speak louder than words, and that is a perfect example of it. And yesterday, she wrote me the sweetest note. How can I ever thank God for sending me these sources of comfort? Another source of strength—and I don't know her name yet—is my secret sis. I couldn't get through this without her. She has been one of the biggest blessings to your mommy. I can't wait to find out who she is to let her know what she has meant to me. Secret sis, thank you for the book. I started reading it yesterday.

The last few days have been wonderful for Mommy. Daddy has been super sweet and has been so reassuring. I love this man that God brought into my life. I feel as if through our last trial, God rekindled something in us. Your life and story have even helped your mommy and daddy.

Your big brother Roman loves to point and touch my belly. When I ask where baby Darcy is, he points to my belly and laughs. He is only two, but he loves you so much too. The other day he actually knelt down and gave you a kiss. I hope you felt it.

Darcy, I can't wait for someday when you meet some of these great people that I speak of. I know that God will bring you to each one and share with you how much they loved you and prayed for you.

You are so special, my sweet child.
Mommy

Wednesday, June 11, 2008

Dear Darcy,

I was so moved today. I went to see your daddy
lead his Bible study, and he was spectacular. He
has been leading it for a while, but today was the
first time I went. I was so blessed by the way the
Holy Spirit moved. I pray that somehow the Lord
relayed the message to you. I am sure that you recognized Daddy's voice. He is definitely blessed to
teach God's Word.

I almost decided to start keeping my journal to
you private. I have talked to Daddy for a few days
about not keeping it public. Daddy wanted me to
pray about it to make sure that is what the Lord
wants, because he felt like I should keep it public. And wouldn't you know it—God answered my
prayer yesterday when I received an e-mail from
Sherree, a lady from our church. I am convinced
now that God wants me to continue keeping this
journal public. He amazes me how He answers our
prayers through His people. Sherree really blessed
me yesterday with her prayers and words of encouragement. This, along with a story that Daddy told
me, was evidence that I should continue to share
my thoughts about you with everyone. He works
with a lady who has two children and told him that
she would have an abortion if she ever got pregnant
again. Then, just a few weeks ago, she told him
that after reading about you, she wouldn't dream of
doing it. If for only that, I am glad that God led us
to do this Web site.

Like I said, Darcy, God is blessing so many people just by your story.
I love you so much.
Mommy

Thursday, June 12, 2008

Dear Darcy,

I must tell you how much your adoptive aunt Mary Cate has been working for you. She has been contacting so many people to pray for you and us. She wants to have so many people praying that there will not be a second that goes by when someone is not praying for you. She is absolutely like family to me. I have never in my life met someone so wonderful. I love that woman so much.

Darcy, most doctors can't help babies with your condition because you have a fatal disease. Mommy has been trying to explore ways to help you if you need it when you are born. Aunt Mary Cate has given me so much hope by finding people who can help. Do I dare to hope? I know that God can do anything, but things look so grim. And what makes me so special that He would give me this miracle? I have been talking to Daddy, who knows me well, and I told him that I feared believing in the unrealistic expectation of you overcoming this. But today I have hope that goes against all of the odds, and it scares me so much. If I start to believe in a miracle or in your overcoming this awful disease and it is not in God's plans, well, I fear that I will crumble. I don't know if I can make it through that. Oh, Lord, give me Your strength. Every day the time draws closer, and I feel myself being more and more anxious. I know God is with me. I am so, so weak, and when He gets me through this, it will be the biggest evidence of His existence. He has given you life and has given me life. We are His. God, please grant me the peace that surpasses all understanding.

I love You, Lord. Thank You for giving me this beautiful child. You have so abundantly blessed me. I know that no matter what happens, You are with me. I know that You will give me strength. It is just hard to understand it now.

I love you, Darcy.
Mommy

Tuesday, June 17, 2008

Dear Darcy,

Mommy loves you so much. Tomorrow I have a doctor's appointment and a sonogram to make sure that you are growing. I can't wait for the update.

A lot has been going on, so I haven't had much time to write. I will write you more tomorrow and let you know about all of the wonderful and strange news. One wonderful praise is that your big sister Mallorie was baptized and took her first Communion on Sunday. Daddy got to baptize her. I was so blessed and thankful to God for His wonderful grace of saving yet another one of your siblings. I will let you know about the other stuff tomorrow.

I love you, my dear, sweet baby. Keep safe, and I hope that tomorrow the doctor tells me that everything is okay.

Sleep tight.
Mommy

Wednesday, June 18, 2008
Good morning, Darcy.

Mommy and Daddy got to see your beautiful face today. You were moving so much when we were looking at you. You were measuring two weeks behind, but you wouldn't know it by looking at Mommy. I am super big. Everything looked good except that your abdomen had some fluid. It is not normal, but the doctor didn't seem too concerned. I love you and still pray for that miracle that only God can give. If not, He will still be glorified. I will never be mad at God, only so thankful that He gave me whatever time He has prepared for me to have with you. I will be sad that you have to battle this, and I always want you to know how much I love you. You will never be forgotten.

Here is the long update for the week that I missed writing to you. Friday we met with the people who will take care of you if Jesus decides to call you home. They have a beautiful area where babies stay. It is the babies' earthly home, and they call it The Garden of Innocence. It is where we can visit you until God resurrects your body. On the way home a lady called about a house that we looked at a year ago and asked if we were still interested. It is big enough for all of your siblings and Mommy and Daddy. We had offered a really low price, so we didn't think any more about it.

Saturday two of your big sisters had sports that they play at the YMCA. Lexy had her best game playing flag football. She is the only girl on the team. She made three touchdowns and two touchdown passes. We then did our normal Saturday morning breakfast at Burger King (Daddy's favorite breakfast place). Then Bella also played her best game at volleyball. She returned a spiked ball. We were all so proud of her and were cheering so loud. We then went to see a movie, and that is when we got the call that the owners had accepted our offer on the big house. Wow, were we surprised! We took your siblings over to see the house, and they loved it. Your brothers especially loved all of the space they had to run around in. They were so happy.

Sunday, Mallie was baptized, and it was Father's Day. We really showered Daddy with a lot of gifts. He was very happy. ☺ After church we showed your siblings where you will live if God calls you home early. The new house is closer to you, and we will visit you all the time. We then went to sign papers on the new house and then came home to start to plan how to get the house ready.

Monday and every day this week we have been working so hard to get the house ready, and that is why I haven't been on the computer much. I hope you understand and know that it doesn't take away the fact that I am constantly thinking about you.

I love you so much, my sweet baby. Mommy will be with you always.

Love,
Mommy

Thursday, June 19, 2008

Dear Darcy,

I didn't sleep well last night, so I got up to answer some e-mails. When Daddy heard me get up, he was so excited to tell me that when he put his arm around me, he felt you moving like crazy. It reminds me of when he wrote to you and told you about how fun it is when he plays and wrestles with your siblings. You finally got some individual time to play with Daddy. He was so excited. I am so glad you got to be with him.

You watched me as
I was being formed
in utter seclusion,
as I was woven together in
the dark of the womb.
You saw me before
I was born.
Every day of my life was
recorded in your book.
Every moment was
laid out before a single
day had passed.

PSALM 139:15-16

I am so glad that Daddy got to feel you move and play with you. It was like you sensed him touching you through my belly. You don't move around a lot, so when you do, it is very special.

We love you very much.
Mommy

Saturday, June 21, 2008

Dear Darcy,

Your sisters had another awesome day with their YMCA sports. It is so fun to see how great they play. They really try hard, and that makes Mommy and Daddy very proud.

We are still trying to get the old house ready for when we move out. Mommy and Daddy took your siblings to a movie and treated them to pizza because they have helped Mommy so much this week. We all worked twelve hours a day, but the whole downstairs is perfect. It looks awesome. It is probably cleaner than when we moved in. The upstairs is our mission for next week. It is hard for Mommy to bend over and scrub the tiles and wood floors, but I did it. Even the grout in the kitchen was an all-day chore, but it is done. There is not so much as a piece of paper out of place downstairs.

I was so glad that we did all of that work, because we were surprised by a visit from some of our old friends. It was so nice to catch up on things. It is so sad that we get so busy with our lives that we haven't seen them in so long. Their kids have gotten so big. They play a lot of sports too. These friends are very good to us, because even though they have a lot of kids, they have always made the effort to visit when they are around here. They said that they are going to pray for you and us. God is so good to us to call so many of His own to pray for us. It was really nice to see them and receive such a wonderful blessing.

That is all that happened today.

Love you,
Mommy

Sunday, June 22, 2008

Dear Darcy,

Mommy feels a little down today. Daddy and Mommy are not on the same page as far as how to handle your treatment when you are born. He says he hasn't decided if we should pursue getting you surgery if you need it. I just can't stand that thought. I want you to be treated like any other precious child that God creates, and if you need surgery for your survival, I think we should get it, even if your life on earth is short. I know that it is expected of me to obey my husband, but how can I not get you medical treatment if you need it? Your life is in God's hands. He gave us doctors to help us. Even Luke, one of Jesus' followers was a doctor. How can I just sit there and let you die if there is a way to save you? Maybe we will not even be given a choice. I know that Daddy loves you very much, but it seems like he is relying on doctors and what they say. And it is all gloom when doctors are telling parents about the effects of trisomy 18. Daddy hasn't spent the time that I have reading about all of the miracles that God has done through babies with your condition. I feel so weak and depleted. I am already having to fight with medical professionals to convince them that you are worthy of saving. I want to go far away so that I can protect you. I feel like I am fighting this battle for you all alone.

Letting you die after birth, without getting you help, would be like abortion, in my eyes. If I don't even give you a fighting chance, it is like my aborting you. The National Institutes of Health (NIH) says, "There is something profoundly troubling about allowing the birth of an infant who is known in advance to suffer from some serious disease or defect. While the prevention of that suffering is attained . . . by eliminating the potential sufferer . . . many would consider it an act of mercy."[5]

Am I wrong for carrying you to term? Am I wrong to protect the very being that God has given me charge of on earth? I pray not! You were given to me for a reason. How can I sit idly by and let the medical professionals discard you because they think you have no quality of life? I wonder if they would do the same if it was their child. I don't know, honey. I just don't know. . . .

Lord, please reveal to me what Your will is. I really don't know what to do. I pray that God will open or close the doors so even someone as ignorant as I am will not be so blind but will see the obvious.

I love you, Darcy. I love you so much!
Mommy

---

[5] National Institute of Child Health and Human Development, *Antenatal Diagnosis*, 1-192, quoted in Eric T. Juengst, "Prenatal Diagnosis and the Ethics of Uncertainty" in *Health Care Ethics: Critical Issues for the 21st Century* (Gaithersburg, MD: Aspen Publishers, 1994), 19.

Wednesday, June 25, 2008

Dear Darcy,

Mommy has realized how selfish I have been and how little faith I have. I have been focusing so much on the pain to come that I have missed out on some of the joy that comes with having you with me now. I need to have faith that I serve the almighty God. He will look out for me as He always has. I know this much: God has prepared me with everything that I need, through my experiences, for a day such as this. He has directed me and guided my every step to get me to this place. Why should I ever doubt that He will provide for my needs now? I have been such a weak Christian. How dare I ever doubt Him? I pray that He can forgive my disbelief. I have always said that I am like Peter, one of Jesus' disciples. He was bold in his faith, but when put to the real test, he denied Christ. That is what I am doing now. I feel so ashamed.

I love the new song that Daddy put on this page because it helped me to realize that I am not alone. I have to see this. God has blessed me with a beautiful husband. And, Darcy, if I have to drink this cup, there is not another person in the world that I would want to drink it with but your daddy. God gave me not only a wonderful husband but also wonderful friends, a wonderful church, and, of course, Himself. I would have never met many, many of the friends I have now if it were not for you. God is good. He is my strength. He is my provider. I get sad for things that may not even happen. I must trust in His Word. We must all love the Lord, not only on the hilltops but also in the valleys of despair. God never promises us that we will not have trials and tribulations. But the good news is that He promises never to leave us or forsake us. God, I pray that You will give me the strength to never deny You or doubt You again.

Darcy, I thank the Lord for giving you to me. I love the Lord for the wonderful people He brought to me because of you. I thank Him for my husband. And most of all, I thank Him for always being there for me, even to this day.

Mommy loves you, Darcy. More than you will ever know. I can't wait to touch your beautiful face.

Thursday, June 26, 2008

Dear Darcy,

Last night was the first time since finding out about your problems that I slept through the night. It feels good to trust that the Lord is going to walk with me and protect me, come what may. I was carrying the cross of what-ifs, and after yesterday I feel a release of this burden. It was a turning point for Mommy. This whole situation has tested and yet strengthened my faith like nothing else I have ever gone through in my life. I thank God for helping me grow in my faith. Once again, it is because of you, my sweet child. I can never give to you what you have given Mommy. God is using you as the vessel to help me grow in faith.

I have started feeling you move more. It is your way of telling Mommy hello. It always seems to happen when I need it most. I know that you are trying to tell me that you are okay and not to worry.

Today is Mommy's lunch date with Daddy, so I can't talk long. Maybe I will write more to you later today.

Until then, I love you.
Mommy

Saturday, June 28, 2008

Dear Darcy,

Today we watched Lexy's last flag-football game. She did well, and her team won, but she wasn't in a lot of the plays. We had a good time supporting her. Chian, Brittany's friend, spent the night last night, so she was able to come with us to support Lexy.

After the game, we decided to go look at our new house again. We found a buyer for our other house and are excited to get moved in. We went there and talked about where we will put all of our things. But we had an event before we stepped into the house. As we walked up the driveway, Mommy tripped on a rock and came tumbling down. Don't worry. I'm all right. Your family, especially Daddy, was so caring and loving and so concerned for Mommy and showed the most compassion you have ever seen. *Not!* We sat there for about ten minutes crying so much from the laughter that

I could not get up. We kept watching and watching the video over and over again and laughing hysterically. It really was funny. Some people might think we're strange, but that is the type of family you have, sweetie. I was so careful to protect you as much as I could. I pulled a leg muscle, but that was about it.

So you see, we are a crazy family who loves to laugh a lot. In fact, we will do just about anything for a laugh. You'll see when you get here.

I love you and can't wait to talk to you more tomorrow.

Good night, dear.
Mommy

july

Tuesday, July 1, 2008

Dear Darcy,

I've decided to share with you some of the blessings that God has given me thus far, as a result
of my knowing your condition early on in the
pregnancy. The blessings I have experienced from
knowing early include having you dedicated, having a 3-D sonogram, loving every single second
that I have you, having maternity photographs
made, celebrating a Mother's Day knowing that
all of my children are alive and well and with
me (it may be the only one that I will have with
you alive), and documenting every day. These are
all things that I would not have done had I not
known. Also, all of my research to help prepare
me, and the Now I Lay Me Down to Sleep organization that will come take pictures. All of these
I would not have known about without previous
knowledge of your condition. The best blessing
that has come to me is the abundance of friends
I have met. These are beautiful people that I may
never have known without you or without knowing of your condition early. God is so good! I
feel so blessed and loved! I am so undeserving to
receive such blessings from the Most High, but
as I have always told you, He is very gracious and
gives to the least of these.

I hear you speak to me the only way you know how, through your movements. You move more and more, and it makes me so happy. I guess I always underestimated the gift that movements are. It is babies' way of communicating with their mommies. I know now how precious it is. Thank you for that gift, little Darcy.

Mommy is very tired. I may go take a nap, and it is still the morning. I hope you are doing well, my sweet daughter.

I love you always.
Mommy

Sunday, July 6, 2008

Dear Darcy,

Mommy is utterly worn out. We have been so busy getting ready for this move. God is gracious for giving me so much to keep me busy, but, *wow*, Mommy is tired.

Daddy had a long break this week. His work gave him a four-day weekend because of July 4. He was off Thursday to Sunday. I love it when Daddy is off for so long. We were able to get a lot of things accomplished while he was home. He organized the whole garage to get it ready for our move, and we finished sorting through the attic stuff. That was a chore. But I think we are almost ready to start packing. We have already packed a lot, but there is a bunch more.

It wasn't all work and no play though. Thursday we worked and then treated the kids to lunch out.

That night we went to a workmate's of Daddy's. They made us hamburgers, and we had good fellowship. They told us about their little girl Hannah, who only lived for six hours after she was born. If God calls you home to live with Him, you could look for her and be her friend. You could tell her that her mommy and daddy still love her so much, even though it has already been four years. But I am sure Jesus already tells her that. Friday we went back to work but were invited to a church member's house to watch fireworks. I was pretty stressed the whole time, trying to watch your fearless two brothers. I hope you weren't scared when you heard all of the loud booms. Daddy loves to pop fireworks, and I had fun watching him. Saturday we met some of our church friends at Burger King for our typical breakfast. Afterward, we cleaned a little and then went to see a movie called *WALL•E*. Your siblings loved it so much. Sunday was church, and afterward we went by our new house to hang out for a while. Your siblings love to run around and play in all of the space. Bryson loves to lie down on the floor with carpet. We have wood floors at our house now, and he has never experienced carpet, so you should see his smile when he brushes his cheek against the floor. Some friends from church came by to see the house too. We had a good time talking and showing them where your room is. You will be sharing a room with Mommy and Daddy, but it is big enough for all three of us.

Well, that is a wrap-up of our week. We have been very busy, but I always think about you and pray that you are okay. I love you, my sweet baby. Mommy is off to bed.

Love,
Mommy

Tuesday, July 8, 2008

Dear Darcy,

Wow! We had a busy day. Today is your biggest brother's birthday. He turned three years old. We started it with our typical birthday doughnut. We could barely wake him up, but when he saw all of the presents wrapped in Spider-Man gift wrap, there was no stopping him. With each new Spider-Man gift he unwrapped, he was equally excited. It was like he had never received a Spider-Man gift! I might have gotten a little disappointed after my sixth or seventh gift that was wrapped the same, but not him.

We soon rushed to get ready for my maternity photo shoot. It is my way of having something tangible to prove that you are real and are a part of our family. It was actually the first professional picture of the whole family, and there you were, kicking like crazy. Don't worry; you were not the only one kicking. Your brothers were too. The lady who took the pictures was so kind and patient. Her name is Debi, and she is the owner of Life's Images Photography.

I can't wait to view the pictures. She donated all of her time and resources for you. It is her way of doing something special for you. What a gift!

People have done so much for Mommy, and it is amazing how God keeps working in my life. I hope and pray that God will bless Debi as much as she has blessed me.

Afterward, we all ate at Burger King as a little birthday lunch for Roman. Debi and her two daughters went with us. It was such a wonderful time.

When Daddy came home, we debated about what to do for Roman. We decided to take him to Chuck E. Cheese. He had a great time. Bryson was also amazed by all of the lights. They had a blast.

Well, now it is bedtime, so I am heading off to bed. We had a long day, and I am sure that you are just as tired as Mommy.

I love you.

Saturday, July 12, 2008

Dear Darcy,

Once again, another busy week. So many things to do and so little time. And I guess that you notice it too, because you have been kicking like crazy. Probably trying to tell Mommy that I need to slow down. Hopefully things will slow down when we get moved.

God has been very good this week. When we saw the doctor on Wednesday, we got to have a 3-D sonogram, and we got to see your beautiful face. You are very petite. The technician seemed to think that your brain cysts have gotten smaller or have gone away. Praise God! We will find out for sure when we see the specialist in two weeks. She didn't mention anything about the holes in your heart, but your heartbeat sounded very strong and was within the normal ranges. We are going back in two weeks for another quick peek to see if we can't get a picture of your whole face. We only got some profiles this time.

Thursday, Daddy and I had our typical lunch date. Friday I took your siblings to McDonald's for lunch, and we came back home and re-covered our couch to get it ready for our new home. Daddy finished it when he came home.

Today we are going to keep packing while Daddy goes through our outside unit to pack some things, and I think he is going to take down the trampoline. Our move date is quickly approaching, and so we are working hard to get things done.

I love you, Darcy. Thank you for always talking to me through your little kicks. I love that.

Mommy

Sunday, July 13, 2008

Dear Darcy,

We had a great day at church. I really can't wait for you to meet some of the spectacular people who love you so much. I was so proud of you and your portrait that I couldn't wait to tell people to go to the site to see it. You are perfectly made, and Mommy is proud.

One wonderful lady, Janice, spent so much time making you some blocks, and they have your name on them. I can't wait to show them to you. People are taking time to make things for you so you will feel special and loved.

Another blessing came from Paula, another lady from church, who gave me a Doppler to borrow so that I can hear your heartbeat anytime I want. I have always wanted to get one but could never afford it. How God has blessed me today! I have already gotten to listen to your heartbeat twice. What a glorious gift.

God has blessed me through His people today with their words of encouragement. Marilyn, from church, told me that she and her husband pray for you every night. God is surrounding you with so many faithful people. There is not a better group of people that I would want to be surrounded by. God is great!

You are God's beautiful gift to me! How I have been blessed because of you. God gave you to me to bless me. I can't wait to see what is in store for me this week!

I love you, Darcy.
Mommy

Tuesday, July 15, 2008

Dear Darcy,

Today we took your big sister Lexy to meet a friend of hers. She used to live across the street, and they were best friends, but then they moved to Nevada. They came into town and asked if Lexy wanted to join them at Sea World and for part of their trip.

So we all loaded up the car and drove her downtown. While there, we had dinner with Sarah (Lexy's friend) and her mom, Sherry. It was good to catch up with them. They moved a year ago, and it was great to hear how God is moving in their lives. We had a wonderful visit. We were already missing Lexy when she left. It won't be the same around here without her, but she is going to have a great time.

Afterward, we came home, and I kept feeling a tightening in my belly. I got out the Doppler and was listening to your heartbeat, and it was stable. I must have just got heartburn or something, because it eventually went away.

We watched a movie as a family and then went to bed.

I love you, Darcy.
Mommy

Friday, July 18, 2008

Dear Darcy,

What an exciting time!

Mommy had the chance to be a voice for babies. I feel so blessed that God gave me the opportunity to share my beliefs. I want you to know that my voice was guided by my undying love for you. You know, I could never have aborted you. I am against abortion, and it is not what God wants. God made you. He made you perfect and just for me. I don't believe that you would have chosen for me to abort you either, even though I know you must struggle.

But the fact that you are still here, when many babies with your condition have already passed by now, is proof that you want to live. At your last sonogram (one and a half weeks ago), you moved and started kicking like crazy when Daddy started talking to you through my belly. That is your way of loving and being a part of him and wanting to be with us and saying, "That's my daddy." You got so excited to know that he was there, speaking to you, and your excitement just thrilled my soul. You want to meet your daddy. You want to be here with us. You want to live.

I know that you will make it to term. You will show everyone that babies, even babies with your condition, want to live. You can be the testimony for life. God is going to use you in a mighty way. I just know it. He already has used you more than He has even used your mommy. I hope I can accomplish with my life what you have with yours (and Mommy has a forty-year head start). Praise God that He has used you for a mighty purpose! Not everyone is given that chance.

I love you, my sweet baby. I love you more than words can even express. . . .

Mommy

Wednesday, July 23, 2008

This may be my last entry. I will continue my diary in writing as we are moving and will not be subscribing to the Internet.

Darcy is doing okay at the moment. She is two

weeks behind, but her organs look good. Except for
a small hernia in her abdomen and the large hole in
her heart, she seems to be doing okay. Please continue to pray for her. I also covet your prayers for
our family. It is a very emotionally charged time.
As the time draws near to Darcy's birth, I struggle
more and more with the fact that some, including
my husband, did not want her. It is hard to accept
under the circumstances.

Thursday, July 24, 2008

Dear Darcy,

How do I make right this wrong? I feel that I have
made your daddy into a monster that he just isn't.
How do I explain this, but that Mommy is dying
inside? My world is shaking apart. I know that
God is in control. I know that He will take care
of everyone, including me. I just don't know how
I can watch you die. How can I be going through
such extremes? I must sound like a maniac. God
gave me your daddy for this time. I know of no
other man who could deal with my insanity. And I
must admit that I have never been this crazy. I have
said it before, but God has really made your daddy
a wonderful man, like no other. No one could walk
this whirlwind life with me but him. And he is so
loving to forgive. I wish that I could be here for
him like he is for me. He has always had an amazing ability to calm me down and love me "despite."
I love him like no other. He loves you very much,
as do I. I hope that I can see through all of this

mess that this can make us stronger and that I will not destroy what God has brought together. I am just not equipped. I need God and your daddy. Thank You, God, for giving him to me.

Darcy, I hope that nothing I have done would ever cause you or anyone else to think that Daddy isn't exactly what he is. He is truly a godly man.

My apologies to all whom I have offended. It was not my intention to hurt anyone. I am sorry for losing faith and for all of my insanity. I love you all and appreciate your support. Please just continue to pray. This weak person needs it now and will need it more as Darcy's arrival comes closer.

I love you, Darcy. You are my sweet and precious child.

Mommy

Thursday, July 24, continued
I feel compelled to share these lyrics of Chris Tomlin's:

Jesus Messiah
He became sin
Who knew no sin
That we might become His Righteousness
He humbled Himself and carried the cross
Love so amazing
Love so amazing

Chorus: *Jesus Messiah*
Name above all names
Blessed Redeemer

Emmanuel
The rescue for sinners
The ransom from Heaven
Jesus Messiah
Lord of all

His body the bread
His blood the wine
Broken and poured out all for love
The whole earth trembled
And the veil was torn.
Love so amazing
Love so amazing

Chorus: *Jesus Messiah*
Name above all names
Blessed Redeemer
Emmanuel
The rescue for sinners
The ransom from Heaven
Jesus Messiah
Lord of all.

All our hope is in You.
All our hope is in You.
All the glory to You, God,
The light of the world.

Chorus: *Jesus Messiah*
Name above all names
Blessed Redeemer
Emmanuel
The rescue for sinners
The ransom from Heaven

Jesus Messiah
Lord of all.

Friday, July 25, 2008

Dear Darcy,

God has provided again! Praise God that He is all the strength we need. When Mommy is weak, He always seems to show and prove to Mommy that He is sufficient.

Mommy has a secret sis, whom God chose for me at the beginning of the year, and she has been a great source of strength for me. She wrote me the most encouraging e-mail today. She has been one of my biggest sources of strength while going through this journey. It is amazing how she has always been there when I needed her most. When God moves her to respond, I can testify that she truly heeds His call. In fact, the other day, when Mommy had her meltdown, she sent me flowers and a precious note. I so needed the encouragement that day. I have been so blessed by her and can't wait to see who she is.

What a wonderful God we serve!

I love you, Darcy.
Mommy

Saturday, July 26, 2008

Dear Darcy,

Today some of my neighborhood friends gave me a farewell party and took me out for lunch. How sweet they were! They treated me to Cheesecake

Factory and got me a one-hundred-dollar gift card to Target to help buy some things for our new house. Wasn't that sweet? We had a very good day, and I so enjoyed it. After lunch I took them to see our new house. It was so much fun. We had a great time!

When we came home, Daddy took Mommy to a movie, and I had contractions throughout the movie. They eventually stopped, but it sure got Mommy scared that you were trying to come early. I want you to stay snug and keep on growing even though I can't wait to see you.

I love you.
Mommy

Sunday, July 27, 2008

Today we had a great time at church. Some very special ladies prayed over me and showered me with love and support. God must have spoken to them because I really needed encouragement today. What an awesome church we have. It is truly one of a kind.

I hope you are still growing and getting bigger.

I love you, sweetie!
Mommy

Monday, July 28, 2008

Dear Darcy,

Today we closed on our houses. We sold one and bought one. Yea! God has provided. I hope that when you get here you love your new home. We are tired, but God is gracious to give us the energy that we need. Ate Brittany is helping so much.

I can't wait to see my precious Darcy.

I love you.
Mommy

august

Tuesday, August 12, 2008

Dear Darcy,

What an exciting couple of weeks we have had! I don't even know where to start. I am sure that you have felt every moment of excitement and exhaustion that has gone on inside of Mommy. Some days I didn't feel you, so I would get out my Doppler and feel the relief that comes from hearing your heartbeat.

After we closed on our homes, things became a whirlwind of emotions and work. We got the keys on the first day, thanks to some last-minute hard work from our finance company. They really worked hard on our behalf because of you, Darcy. That was another miracle that we received in this whole journey. We started moving in the first day and preparing our new house for moving in.

Tuesday, Brittany and I kept the boxes coming as Daddy had to go to work. Wednesday, Daddy took off, and that began the big journey of transporting our things to the new house. Your family from church was so eager and ready to help. They actually got so many things moved that we were able to stay in our new house. They had our kitchen up and functioning and the beds up, so we were excited to be there in our new home. Thursday we hung up the window blinds, and Friday about fifty people showed up to move the rest of our things. What can I say but that God has tremendously blessed us with such a gracious church family.

Since then, we have unpacked boxes and got things ready. We just got Internet today, so I am able to talk to you again through your site. I have missed writing to you and sharing all of the blessings surrounding us. I have received numerous words of encouragement and blessings. Because of you, my blessings have soared and increased beyond words.

I thank everyone for their prayers for you and our family. Everyone has blessed us tremendously.

We go to the doctor tomorrow to see how you are growing.

I love you, Darcy.
Mommy

Monday, August 18, 2008

Dear Darcy,

Mommy has had a crazy week. I have been shaken, and I have been blessed.

After I wrote to you last week, I quickly learned that a friend of mine, whom I met on the Internet and who was also expecting a T18 baby, lost her in the womb. She was about eight weeks younger than you are. Mommy got really sad. I was starting to get more relaxed, because Daddy and Ate Brittany kept telling me how they think God will let you be with us for a while. The news really gave Mommy a reality check, and I felt a bit sick this last week. I know that the prognosis is not good for you, but we have had thousands of people praying for you, and I had begun feeling a lot of hope. My friend and I have been praying for both you and her baby, and we had such hope of y'all being with us on earth. But God is in control. She explained what a beautiful experience it was to hold her baby girl, despite the sadness it brought. We both know that she and you will be in a much better place, and for that we are so thankful to God.

Although the news came as a big shock, I also had a lot of blessings. Daddy and Mommy have been getting closer than ever. God has been so gracious in bringing us closer and not letting this trial come between us. Lola also came down and bought us a new play set for the backyard. It was her contribution to our new house. I was talking to Daddy about how nice it would be for you to experience it. He once again reminded me that nothing here on earth can compare with the joys in store for you in heaven. And he is right. I do picture you running alongside your sisters and brothers and having fun though. If God blesses us to have you come home with us, I promise to take you outside with me and sit on the bench so you can see the play set and watch your siblings.

Last week's doctor's appointment was typical. We heard your heartbeat and took the typical vitals. Everything was fine, but Daddy and I went away from it thinking that your heartbeat sounded a little slow. I know it is typical for heartbeats to fluctuate, but since you have this condition, we take it a bit more seriously. But you have been moving around a lot, and when I want to hear your heartbeat at home, I just get out my Doppler.

I love you so much.
Mommy

Tuesday, August 19, 2008

Dear sweetheart,

How do I even begin today's journal? Things were going so well. Today Daddy and I celebrated our nineteenth anniversary. We had a lovely lunch at our favorite Thai restaurant, and Daddy planned a lovely dinner at an exclusive restaurant. On the way to dinner, your uncle Kevin called and told Daddy that my mom (your grandma) had passed away. She loved you very much, Darcy. I guess Jesus wants your grandma to greet and welcome you into heaven. Your Meema will be there waiting.

Darcy, you will have so many family members and friends awaiting your arrival. You will never be alone. With Jesus at your side, you will never be alone, and your life in heaven will be so full of love.

I love you, Darcy. Keep snug. I can't wait to meet you in person, my precious child.

Mommy

Wednesday, August 20, 2008

Dear Darcy,

No one can ever convince me that things happen by coincidence. God controls everything, and nothing happens outside the will of the Lord Most High. Even though things may seem dark and gray, He still comes to comfort us in the valleys. He is truly the great Comforter.

Daddy always says (including today at his Bible study) that he is not surprised but is amazed by God. That is becoming more and more evident. Today, our new neighbor Leila (not knowing what had happened) brought food over. She had more than what she and her husband could eat and decided to bless us. It amazes me how God provides. Why now? Why today? I wonder what would happen if God's people did not heed the call of the Holy Spirit. I guess He would find other ways to provide.

Brittany just came home with a beautiful present from Nicole, someone she babysits for. It was the most beautiful set of candleholders, and one had this verse on it, which she also wrote in the card: "The joy of the LORD is your strength" (Nehemiah 8:10). What a perfect time to reflect on those words. Once again, the Lord provides for everything we need and at every moment.

I reflect through the years and wonder, *Why me?* Why would God choose to bless me in this way? I am nothing special. In fact, I am the least worthy of these blessings. And even through these trials, He showers me with mercy, grace, love, and blessings. I can't even explain how, while down in the valley, I feel this way. It is something I have never felt before. It is completely new to me. How can I feel this peace at this time? God is constantly reassuring me that everything is going to be okay. I must lean not on my own understanding but take comfort in the fact that He is in control. I cannot live in a spirit of fear, but of power, and of love, and of a sound mind. God is good!

I love you, Darcy!
Mommy

Monday, August 25, 2008

Dear Darcy,

We just got back from our busy and hectic weekend. Your grandma had a beautiful service. Thanks to your uncle Kevin, who planned and organized it, things went wonderfully. You would be very proud of him. He showed such great courage through the whole thing. There were a lot of beautiful flowers. Uncle Kevin chose some beautiful clothes and jewelry, and your grandma looked so young and so good.

During the funeral I got to meet some church members from Merit Baptist Church who have been praying for you. It was so wonderful to put faces to these wonderful people who send me letters and tell me how they are praying for you every day. They also donated their facilities, services, and food to our family. Once again, God showed Himself in a mighty way.

It is good to be home. We are all tired and are going to get some sleep.

I love you.
Mommy

Wednesday, August 27, 2008

Dear Darcy,

Everyone get ready to help me praise our almighty God! After today's appointment with Dr. Kirshon, the trisomy specialist, I left speechless.

We had a normal visit with Dr. Ritter in the morning. Daddy and Mommy had lunch at Nit Noi and then headed over to Dr. Kirshon for our level II ultrasound. During the ultrasound, Dr. Kirshon kept talking about how active you were and how your heart seems to be tolerating your condition. Daddy started asking questions about your heart, about whether it was operable. Dr. Kirshon said, "Yes, but not with trisomy 18 babies." He also mentioned that he didn't know of anyone who would operate on babies like you and that in all of his experience, he has never seen a baby born with T18 that survived longer than twenty-four hours after birth.

Daddy asked about your brain cysts, and Dr. Kirshon said they are gone. Daddy asked about your hernia, and the doctor said he didn't see it. Despite the holes, your heart seems to be doing okay now too. As we were discussing these miracles, we could see a change in the doctor's expression and tone. So Daddy asked the big question. He asked the doctor, "In your experience (he has had many trisomy babies under his care), how many babies with T18 have made it to thirty-four weeks?"

Well, the doctor didn't answer the question but

rather said that we can be "cautiously optimistic." This gave Mommy and Daddy tremendous hope.

We are all witnessing what you are going through and are astonished by the power of God and His miracles! Now here is the biggie! For the first time in this journey, we heard the most miraculous and encouraging words from Dr. Kirshon. He said that if you made it through the first twenty-four hours and you were showing signs of wanting to live, we could take you to Texas Children's Hospital, where doctors will help you live. *Wow*—did Mommy's eyes pop out! That was the very first time I had heard anything that promising. At first, both of your doctors were so adamant that doctors don't operate on babies with your condition. This was the first time we heard optimistic words from a medical professional. It is not a cure, but at least it gives us hope that you may be able to be with us to enjoy your family for a longer time than we expected. I also know that babies with T18 who do get surgery live longer because doctors will actually work on them.

Praise God! I want to give you every chance that I would give all of your siblings. Mommy was so needlessly worried about this. God is leading and directing our every step. He will provide according to His will. All things are possible with God. And if you don't make it to forty-eight hours, that will be in God's plan too. I really needed to hear some encouraging news today, and that is how God blessed me.

Every time you say hello to me by kicking and

moving around, I just rub my belly and tell you how much your mommy loves you. It is our special way of talking. God has been so gracious.

I love you, Darcy.
Mommy

september

Wednesday, September 3, 2008

Dearest Darcy,

I don't even know where to begin. I received such blessed news today. It always amazes me how God works and brings people into your life. Nothing is by coincidence. I am truly humbled by the generosity of others. One of my errands yesterday was to go to the bank. The teller was busy helping another customer, so she referred me to Tiffany. (Remember, nothing happens by accident.) Well, as Tiffany started helping me, we found that we had a lot in common. She is expecting to give birth at any time (like Mommy), she sells Mary Kay (like Mommy), and she lost her last baby at six months. It is so unnatural for parents to outlive their children.

It was hard to hear about her suffering, but God brought her to me for a special reason. She called me today to express that she wanted to do something special for you. So she decided to do a Mary Kay Satin Hands Pampering Set benefit in your name. She is going to donate the profits to your memorial fund. When she expressed this to her sales director, the sales director wanted to do the same thing. So they are setting up events, for anyone in their unit who would like to be a part of them, to earn money to help the causes set for your memorial fund. What an absolutely gracious and generous gift! This is yet another example of how God continues to bless you and me through His people. I am truly in awe. How could I ever thank these people for their generosity? And they are doing it for you, sweetie!

God is so good! He never leaves us, even in the darkest valleys.

I love you, Darcy. Because of you, God has revealed Himself to me like never before.

Mommy

Tuesday, September 9, 2008

Dear Darcy,

You have come a long way, my sweet child! Most babies with your condition do not make it to this point (thirty-six weeks tomorrow). God has truly amazed me by His sovereignty through your life. You make Mommy so proud! This morning you were just jumping and dancing all around Mommy's belly. I cherish every movement, and oh how relieved I feel every time you assure me that you are still here with me. You are truly a beautiful gift from God!

Even when I walk through the darkest valley, I will not be afraid, for you are close beside me. Your rod and your staff protect and comfort me.

PSALM 23:4

Today is exactly one month till your due date. While you are inside the warm and cozy womb that God has provided for you, that is when I feel most safe with you here with me. It is as we draw closer to your due date that uncertainties creep in. I feel a constant uneasiness about what is to come. As the day approaches, I have to admit that I feel more and more anxious about the next few days or weeks. It is hard for mommies to remain hopeful when we are left with the unknown about the safety and security of our babies' future. It makes it easier to cope knowing that our children belong to the Lord, no matter what. It is almost unbearable for those who know that they won't have their babies for long. It is not that I am ungrateful for the undeserved time that God has given you to me, but I fear how I'm going to ache and long for you when you are gone. I know what a much better place you will be in, and I know that God will be here for me when you are gone. I don't know how unbelievers make it during times like this.

Darcy, I just want you to know how much I dearly love you and that I would love to have you here with me forever. We are not guaranteed tomorrow, so we must be thankful for today. And I am so thankful that our most loving God gave me the sweetest baby and the most wonderful gift of knowing you.

You were woven together by His hands in perfect form. Thank You, Lord, for this most perfect gift!

I love you, my sweet baby. I will always love you. You will never be forgotten. And no matter how short our time together on earth may be, one glorious day we will have eternity to praise the

Almighty together, free of pain and worry. I look forward to that day.

Mommy

Thursday, September 18, 2008

Dear Darcy,

Things have been a little crazy here. During the past nine days we have had a hurricane, lost power, water, a tree, a fence, the Internet, and use of our cell phones. Add to the mix the fact that your big sister had a birthday and Daddy's birthday is tomorrow, and well, we have been quite busy. We have been so blessed that our situation was not as bad as others'. Our surrounding cities have been flooded and pounded, but we are safe, and God had His hedge of protection around us. He loves us so much. He spared us from having any injuries. We have been so busy cleaning up the yard and debris and trying to cut down the big tree that fell. God made trees very strong and the roots very strong. Daddy has been working every day to try to remove it.

Despite the widespread devastation, we tried to make the best of it and make it a time of blessing and bonding. That is how your family is.

I feel your time is coming near. I was having a bunch of contractions last night, coming three minutes apart. When I lay down to go to sleep, they stopped. Maybe I just overdid it today. My anticipation and anxiety are growing like my belly.

Daddy went back to work today. Mommy is

going to go get ready for our lunch date. I hope our favorite Thai restaurant is open. Many places are still closed.

I love you, Darcy. I go to the doctor today to make sure you are okay.

Mommy

Saturday, September 27, 2008: Day 1

Welcome to the world, little Darcy!

Darcy is here! She was born at 9:52 p.m., weighing in at 4 pounds, 7 ounces and measuring 17 inches long. She gets her height from her daddy. She is stable and seems to be doing well. She is not feeding well, but we are working on it. She is the most beautiful, petite baby I have ever seen. She is very calm and sweet natured. She didn't need oxygen and had no trouble breathing. I am so proud of her. She had numerous visitors. The hospital staff is extremely helpful and patient. I could not ask for a better crew. We had the most wonderful photographers come and take photos of her. I can't wait to see them. The kids loved her from the start. They all wanted to hold her constantly. Our pastor, his family, our church family, and friends all came to greet Darcy as she came into the world.

God is so gracious and merciful for allowing us to experience this beautiful time with this sweet baby.

We will see how things progress and keep everyone informed.

Thanks for all of the prayers.

Tracy

Sunday, September 28, 2008: Day 2

We came home today! Another miracle from God that the doctors said wouldn't happen. What can I say? Darcy is perfect!

Brittany went to pick up Lola from the airport. I found out today that Lola is in denial about the severity of Darcy's condition. Since there has been an abundance of miracles, Lola thought that Darcy is a perfect, healthy child. I had to remind the kids that Darcy is a very sick baby and we need to treat her as such. They, like Lola, see her as this perfect little angel who overcame the odds to live a normal life. The reality is that her time with us is short. Because her cells are all messed up, she and life are, as the doctors put it, "incompatible."

However long God wills for you to stay, little Darcy, we will enjoy every moment with you. Ever seen the movie *The Bucket List*? Well, we have a "Darcy List" of things that we think you should experience before you return to Jesus. Here are some of those things:

> Feel the warm Texas sun on your face
> Ride the swing with Mommy
> Ride the motorcycle with Daddy
> Go to church and meet your church family
> Dance with Mommy and Daddy
> Get a sticker tattoo
> Receive a million kisses

It's a beautiful day today. I just gave birth yesterday without any pain medication, and I am tired. After a nap, we'll start checking things off your list.

I love you, Darcy! Happy Second Birthday! ☺
Mommy

Monday, September 29, 2008: Day 3
What a blessing you are, Darcy!

You have filled our home with your presence, and we are honored to have such a distinguished heavenly visitor. I hope God booked your return trip for a long time from now.

Your Lola (grandma) came yesterday, and your uncle Jet came today. Your auntie Joy comes tomorrow. They came from Dallas and California to see, hold, and kiss you. They will be a big help to us as we transition you to your temporary home. Our church family has arranged for us to receive meals every day this week. Can you believe their love and support for your family? What a wonderful church we have!

[Jesus said,] "Let the children come to me. Don't stop them! For the Kingdom of God belongs to those who are like these children." . . . Then he took the children in his arms and placed his hands on their heads and blessed them.

MARK 10:14-16

We saw your pediatrician, Dr. Yut, today and discussed many options. He pledges to do whatever we wish for you, and we are thankful for that. He is a nice man. You are blessed to have him on your side. Please be patient with us, Darcy. You were in danger of dehydration, so one of the options includes feeding you through a tube. But that should be good, because you won't have to work so hard to get food into your stomach. Don't worry, however, because we will let you taste stuff once in a while. What did you think of your cake? Cakes and delicious meals will come your way every day this week from your church family. Cool, huh? All for you, my love.

Gotta get your sleeping area ready.

I love you, my sweet.
Mommy

Tuesday, September 30, 2008: Day 4

Late last night and today were very scary days for us. You had bouts of apnea last night. Today, after your photo shoot with Ms. Bobbi, the Now I Lay Me Down to Sleep (NILMDTS) photographer, you turned gray several times. We were so afraid that today was the day you would return to heaven, so we had to stay awake. We thought we had everything planned, and we thought we were prepared to deal with your condition. We realize now that we'll never be prepared. We love you so much, and it breaks our hearts to know what you have to go through. When you began turning gray every thirty minutes, we called your Pastor Dan and his wife, Ms. Peggy, to come and see you. Since they are also registered nurses, it was great to have them here. Your daddy called Dr. Yut, but he was out. His backup, however, was Dr. Kahney, your daddy's doctor. I described your situation to Dr. Kahney, and he arranged hospice and other logistical stuff and assured us that he was there if we needed him.

We had a few more items that we wanted to check off your Darcy List, so we hurried up and did them, just in case you had to go. We placed a "cutie" tattoo on your right arm, you took a bath with Mommy, and you danced with me and your daddy. We also were able to check off the scariest item on the list—you rode with Daddy on his little motorcycle.

Well, you beat your challenges today, including the motorcycle ride, and made it to your party. At 9:52, shortly after another photo shoot with Ms. Shona, we celebrated your fourth birthday with Mommy, Daddy, your siblings, your Lola, Uncle Jet, and Auntie Joy. I think we are all going to gain weight. ☺ Your photos are great, Darcy. I will post several of them on your Pics page.

I love you, Darcy.

Happy Birthday!
Mommy

october

Wednesday, October 1, 2008: Day 5

Happy Fifth Birthday, my love!

I am so thankful to God for giving you the
strength to survive another of my sleepless nights
of anticipating what I've been fearing. How can
I sleep when my baby is so close to leaving me?
But I am so tired, and my body gives up despite
my fight to stay awake. Your daddy and big sister
Brittany have been so good to share the hours
with me.

You struggled so much today. Daddy and
Mommy were so worried. It is very hard to accept
things that you think you have prepared for. I
think you got so hungry that when you tasted
Mommy's milk for the first time, you tried to
drink too fast and aspirated some of it. I hope it
doesn't lead to pneumonia. That is an awful disease and causes many of the deaths of infants with
your condition. Mommy was very sad because I
wanted to help you so much, but there was nothing I could do. You cried for hours, which is bad
because you already have issues that make your
oxygen levels low. You had eaten so very little all
week that when you were eating fast, I was happy
that you were finally eating. I wasn't even thinking
about the possibility that you would aspirate. It

hurts me so much to think that I caused your suffering.

Dr. Kahney arranged for Houston Hospice. We anxiously waited for them to come. Every second they were not here was almost a decision to take you to Texas Children's via ambulance. Daddy finally had enough and called them so that they would know that it was urgent and we needed them quickly. When Kristie, the hospice nurse, finally got here, she told Daddy and me about the ways that they were going to help you. After getting more advice from Dr. Yut, we agreed to proceed with hospice. When you get stronger, we will see about getting you more help. But for right now, you are just too small, and we want to make you stronger and more comfortable.

Thank God for Kristie! She calmed our anxieties by explaining the possible causes of your crying. She explained that you are a baby who will continue to show typical baby things, like getting gas and having the need to be hugged and patted. Kristie placed an NG (nasogastric) tube inside you and taught us how to use it. She ordered oxygen and medications as well. We were ecstatic that we were finally able to give you much more than 3 ml of food a day! We are looking forward to seeing you gaining back all the weight you lost. I promise to fight the temptation to feed you too quickly.

Pastor Ted, Erin, and Nubia came to visit you while we converted our bedroom into a hospital. You were still very weak and not doing too well. While Kristie helped you, especially with feeding, you slowly but surely got a little better. We had many more visitors today. By the time Kristie came by, you had pretty much recovered and were a lot better. I am so glad that food can finally fill your belly, Darcy! You haven't pooped and peed in so long that I'm looking forward to changing diapers—many of them!

One great thing that we accidentally discovered helped prevent your blueness. During Kristie's visit, while Daddy held you, he noticed how you calmed down when he let your head tilt back over his forearm. It was evident that that position allowed you to take in air more easily. That revelation convinced us that your blueing was caused by lack of air and made us even more excited about getting the oxygen machine.

At around eight in the evening, the grandfather of a trisomy 18 baby who had recently returned to Jesus called us. It was such a blessing to hear first-hand what they went through with their grandson, Jace. Our conversation gave us hope that you could potentially be with us for weeks. It made us feel so much better to know of more ways to help you in your fight to stay with us longer.

The oxygen machine and medications came after ten. The plan was to give you oxygen when you turned blue, but since discovering ways to keep air coming, we'll just use it to keep your air clean all the time. ☺ Your meds included morphine. I'm hoping all we'll need is the gas medicine.

You've stopped crying a lot by midnight. You must have been very hungry. Your color is starting to get better. I'm praying for a better day tomorrow. I need to know that there is a light around the corner and the corner is close by. Everything about me aches. I know that God gave you to us for a short time, but I don't want to give you back to Him. It just seems so wrong.

I love you, Darcy. It's hard to explain the love I feel for you, even though I've just met you. Your daddy and I will fight to keep you comfortable. We will also fight to keep you here as long as you want to be.

I'm so tired. Tonight will bring its challenges, but I hope it won't be like the past few nights. I am leaning on Psalm 30:3-5: "You brought me up from the grave, O LORD. You kept me from falling into the pit of death. Sing to the LORD, all you godly ones! Praise his holy name. For his anger lasts only a moment, but his favor lasts a lifetime! Weeping may last through the night, but joy comes with the morning."

May you rest well tonight, my dear Darcy.
Mommy

Thursday, October 2, 2008: Day 6

Dear Darcy,

You are six days old today. You have brought your family so much joy! How God has blessed us through you! I am so thrilled that you are doing much better since your feeding tube was placed in you and we have an oxygen supply in case you have those blue spells.

We have been going through the Darcy List. So far, you have your nails painted, you got tattooed, rode the swing with Mommy, rode the motorcycle with Daddy, had a bubble bath with Mommy, and went to McDonald's with your family. There are a few more items. Tomorrow is the Right-to-Life banquet. I'll get your best dress ready for that.

Good night, Darcy. I love you more than I can express.

Mommy

Friday, October 3, 2008: Day 7

What a difference a day makes, Darcy!

You are still here and seem to be strong. You were certainly strong enough to make it to the Right-to-Life Celebration of Life banquet. We dressed you up in your best duds and took you and Brittany to the formal event. We had some delays getting there, but we got there anyhow and got to meet some interesting people. We met Mary Jo Graham, the wife of Dr. Joseph Graham, founder of Texas Right-to-Life. We also met Elizabeth Graham, the current leader of this wonderful organization that fights for kids like you.

We stayed for just a few minutes, however, because the fanfare was too much for you. You had some blue spells. Thank God for the oxygen bottle! When we got home, we retreated to the bedroom and exhaled. Seemed like you were so glad to be home.

Attend the Texas Right-to-Life banquet: Check!

Tomorrow morning we will go to Burger King and get that Darcy List item checked off. The BK Croissan'wich is your daddy's favorite breakfast item. We never miss that Saturday morning family breakfast.

Good night, Darcy. We'll keep the oxygen on for you.

Sweet dreams, my love.
Mommy

Saturday/Sunday, October 4 and 5, 2008: Days 8 and 9

Oh, my sweet little Darcy,

Yesterday I wrote, "What a difference a day makes." I suppose I could write the same sentence again. But, Darcy, you took a turn for the worse today, and I have never shed so many tears.

The day started at Burger King; then we went straight home because that short trip made you tired. You seemed different today . . . weak and not as responsive as yesterday. You also took long naps and didn't remind us about your hunger. I was worried all day about what might be wrong this time.

The Smiths came over to help celebrate your eighth birthday. We all had a great time telling stories, talking about you, and even looking at old pictures and videos. We laid you on the bed and had the sweetest time with you. For the first time, you were wide-eyed and looked around the room at all of us. It was the most beautiful moment I've had with you so far. Daddy and I took turns reading the Bible to you, and you seemed to respond by the way you looked at us.

But exactly one hour after your birthday party, while in the middle of a feeding, you turned blue and went limp. My heart sank to see the thing I feared the most. Before then, you recovered after a few seconds. Those seconds came and went, however, and there you were. Lifeless. Daddy placed you on the floor and immediately performed CPR on you. I tried what I could to help, but whatever I did wasn't enough to make me feel I helped at all. You didn't breathe, and your pulse slowed to almost a halt. Ten minutes went by so quickly, but we did not give up. How could we?

When Bill and Terri came in the room, we all called out your name and prayed and worked on you as best as we knew how. It was when we said that you needed to come to church tomorrow that you took a long breath and let out a silent cry. What a fighter you really are, Darcy! But I was still anxious. Will you make it to your final Darcy List item, which is go to church, or is that church service *the* church service in the presence of our Lord Most High?

An hour went by, and you did not look good, Darcy. We sensed that tonight was going to be your last, so we gathered and said our good-byes. I have never seen our family weep so much. We took a lot of pictures of you with your siblings. They all took

93

turns kissing you and telling you how much you mean to them. We love you so much, Darcy, that we don't want your short visit to end. It hurt me so much to see all my babies cry.

It was shortly after midnight, while your sisters were saying good-bye, that you did it again. You suddenly turned blue and went limp, just like you did the hour before. Oh, Darcy. How I hated to see you suffer! Daddy told your siblings to leave the room because he wanted to protect them from seeing you in that condition. You turned blue faster than before, and your temperature sank to 94.1. Daddy and I really thought you would not make it the second time around, but you did! There was no doubt that you are truly a fighter, Darcy! By this time, our grief was mixed with compassion. You seemed to suffer so much both times we resuscitated you. We secretly prayed that God would take you quickly and without any pain. We cleaned your limp body up and dressed you in one of Mommy's favorite dresses. We were getting you ready for your homegoing, Darcy. You are the most beautiful thing I have ever seen! Oh, how my heart aches for you. Please, God. Not yet. Please.

A few minutes after you recovered, Andrew, the hospice nurse, arrived and assessed your condition. Your heart was racing, and your body was cooler. You looked even worse than before. My entire being was hurting! If I had a choice between a perfect child and you, I would always choose you, my sweet little Darcy. You are my baby, and I never want to let you go. Andrew told us that we should say our good-byes because after two resuscitations, the odds were monumentally stacked against you. So we did. In the middle of our second round of good-byes, however, you did it again. It was round three, Darcy, and we wondered how much energy you had left to keep on fighting. This time, Daddy asked the nurse to take over. You turned blue in a matter of seconds. It did not look good for the first minute, but after about two more minutes, you came back to life . . . yet again.

You were so exhausted after the third round that Andrew really doubted you would survive a fourth round. So he stayed much longer and waited for an hour. In the meantime, we said more good-byes and shed more tears. We read more Bible verses to you. At one point, you smiled as Isabella read. It was such a refreshing gift, Darcy. Thank you!

Well, it is now 4:00 a.m., and you are still here. Andrew checked your vitals and cautiously expressed how amazed he is at your staying power. But we all know where the power came from. Oh, Lord, when will You take Your little evangelist home? Is her work done? I am weary. Exhausted. I have never felt so low in my entire life. But, Lord, I still trust in You. I beg You to keep my little baby from suffering anymore. If You have to take her, please do it quickly and painlessly.

Daddy is getting the bed ready. You will sleep on my chest while I take a nap. I have accepted what-ever God wills for you. I will sleep and rest in the Lord.

This all feels like a terrible dream. I am hoping

that I wake up and everything will have been just that—a terrible dream.

Sunday, October 5, 2008: Update!

You survived the rest of the night but were too weak to go to church, and Daddy and I feared taking you would be the last straw. We didn't understand how God would have laid on our hearts all of the things that we felt we needed to experience with you and yet this one main thing wasn't going to happen. Daddy and I kept praising God for allowing us to have accomplished all of the things on your Darcy List and thought that the last thing, going to church, meant that God was going to have you go to church today in heaven. Well, that didn't happen. I know that I have told you, sweet baby, that we have the absolutely most caring and loving church here on earth, but we really do. They knew how important that last thing on your Darcy List was to us, and so our pastors put together an evening church service and brought it to you. They came to our home and set things up and praised God for being gracious and merciful to us during this last week. It was the most beautiful service I have ever been to, honoring God for your life.

Another thing. Right before the service, we read from your blog page about a woman who came back to the arms of God after losing her faith and that your life had impacted her to the point of returning to Him. I wondered, *What a wonderful thing that God used you to do that for Him.* Here you are, a babe—you can't even speak words—and yet you led someone to the Lord through your life alone. God can bring people to Him without one word even being said. We read the woman's blog entry during the service. It was beautiful!

After the service, Terri (the wife of one of the elders) came over to help take care of you. She worked as a nurse for seventeen years, and she wanted to help us. She got to celebrate your ninth birthday with us and actually stayed till after four in the morning so that Daddy and Mommy could get some rest. Giving up her own rest and time with family, just to tend to you, Darcy.

Darcy, you are an amazing testimony of the one and true living God. God is real and is living and talking through you, my sweet child. I count it all blessing to be a part of this wonderful journey and to get to see the face of God through my special delivery.

I love you and pray that God will shield you through any pain or sorrow. Sometimes I see so much pain and agony when you are having one of your sick spells, and it breaks my heart. But one day there will be no more sorrow and no more pain, my sweet child. Your life is in God's hands, and we must walk the journey that He has set forth for us.

I love you.
Mommy

Sunday, October 5, 2008

Ms. Terri (who we call Aunt Terri) was the first to come and stay all night with you. Ms. Kristy

Bailey asked on Friday, but Mommy was still nervous about you being away from Mommy overnight. She will probably have another chance soon. What a great church family we have!

Monday, October 6, 2008: Day 10

Dear Darcy,

Today was a normal day, with you sleeping most of the time. I had to wake you up for feedings because they sometimes make you restless and upset, but you have to eat. I have kept with the feeding schedule that Terri set up for you. I think it works better for your little tummy, and I notice that you don't have as many of the blue spells, so we will stick to that for a while. The hospice nurse Kristie and the social worker, Les, came by today. You seem to have stayed the same weight since Friday, which is good considering how we took out your feeding tube for hours on Sunday when we gave you CPR. You didn't eat for a whole twelve hours, but you still maintained your weight on Monday. Good girl!

I keep thinking about yesterday, after your third resuscitation, how Daddy and I couldn't bear to put you through that turmoil anymore, and yet God knew that He was going to rescue you and we wouldn't need to do it anymore. It truly is a miracle that you are still here with us. Many people keep telling me how most babies in the fragile state that you are in would not have survived the first two, let alone a third round of CPR. And yet here you are. It is a huge testimony of what a mighty and awesome God we serve!

We celebrated your tenth birthday. A few minutes after your party, Pastor Ted called and blessed us like we have not been blessed thus far. He shared with us what a family from our church offered to us. The precious act of this special family is beyond what anyone else has done so far. It was the most sacrificial and gracious offering made to you. We don't know if it is even possible, sweetie, but when Daddy and Mommy heard of what this family had offered to us, we were so broken by the offering, and it can only be described as the most humbling, undeserved gift that has ever been presented to us. This gift was the gift of a heart. A heart for you. This other family is also expecting a precious baby girl soon who is not expected to survive, like you. But we serve a mighty God, and anything is possible. You are an example of this, Darcy. However, if their precious baby goes to be with Jesus, Darcy, they said that they would give you her heart, knowing that is the biggest problem you have with your organs. And her heart is strong. Like I said, I don't know if it is even possible due to your condition or if you are even strong enough to have a transplant, but what a blessing to have someone who will grieve like we do offer you every chance at living, through their sacrifice.

I have never been humbled this way in my entire life. I have never seen the power of God work this way, ever. I am in awe of His greatness!

It may seem as if these miracles that have

happened through your life and on this journey are too good to be true. But they are a true testament to what we have experienced. Darcy, God chose to use you to demonstrate His power. It has and continues to be the most remarkable experience of my life.

Later that evening, Pastor Dan and his eldest son, Chris, came over to take care of you all night so that Daddy and Mommy could rest. Pastor Dan and his wife, Peggy, are nurses and know exactly what to do. How our needs are being met through our loving Father in heaven and because our church is obedient to listen to the Lord when He moves them. Our church and the sacrifices the people have made to help us in our time of need are too numerous to count. Thanks just doesn't seem enough. Families sacrificing their time and resources to cook, clean, take care of you, and take pictures of you. Giving their spouses, moms, dads, sisters, and brothers so that they can minister to our needs.

God is so great! He is the Most High! He does supply all of our needs! And He will never leave or forsake us! These words have never been more true than they are for me today! Amen!

I love you, sweet Darcy!
Mommy

Tuesday, October 7, 2008: Day 11

Dear Darcy,

Today, another sweet lady from our church, Ms. Colleen, had your big brothers come over to her house to play so that I could take care of you. They had a very good time. You were very good, and your big sisters were able to get some homeschool done. Daddy was also able to go to work for a little while.

Things went very well today.

I love you.
Mommy

Wednesday, October 8, 2008: Day 12
Hi, Darcy.

Today your daddy and I took you to my ob-gyn clinic at Women's Healthcare Affiliates to meet Dr. Ritter and the rest of the staff. The staff members at the clinic have been following your story and heard firsthand how things were going with Mommy while you were inside me. Anne and I always exchanged stories about our families. We laughed and cried at almost every visit. Misty called me often to make sure I was doing well. While we were there, you opened your eyes. I hope you got to see all of them.

The trip to the clinic was tough for you, so we dreaded driving back home. It was a good visit. Although it was rough, I'm sure you were glad to have met those who worked to keep you healthy while you were inside me. We may return to see Dr. Ritter some other day.

Thursday, October 9, 2008: Day 13

Dear Darcy,

Today was your actual due date, and yet I am so glad that I have had you for almost two weeks already. What can I say besides, "God is great!"

Uncle Kevin called today, and somehow he did not receive the message that you were even here yet. He was asking about you because October 9 stuck in his head. He was so happy to hear that you are with us and doing well.

Dr. Krauter, the Houston Hospice doctor, came by to check on you. She was super nice. This hospice center is great, and we feel blessed that God led us to them. I keep thinking back to when you were first diagnosed and when abortion was offered as an alternative. I can't help but think of all of the blessings we would have lost if we had chosen that route. The truth is, having an abortion does not make this journey painless. Neither does carrying to term. Pain is always going to be part of the decision. The difference is, choosing to abort you would have denied me the wonderful blessing of knowing you and all of the blessings that have come from your birth. Just look at the pictures and you would see that.

I've also realized that hospice has been a critical part of the support that I never knew was available. Hospice is not only about death, as I once thought. It is about being provided a better quality of life for you and your family that is as comfortable as possible for the remaining time you have left on earth.

Hopefully soon we can move on to more corrective care when you are stronger and your condition becomes more stable. I really underestimated the invaluable support that comes from hospice. We thought it was only available for older people. We were wrong.

Some hospices, such as Houston Hospice, offer prenatal care for families in situations similar to ours. They offer counseling, volunteers to help where needed, and nursing staff to check on vitals and medical conditions in a very compassionate way. The best part is that you are home with your family being loved and cared for while being given the medical attention you need to stay comfortable. Thank God for the folks at Houston Hospice. I dread even thinking about the alternative.

Friday, October 10, 2008: Day 14

Hi, Darcy.

Your daddy is typing this entry for me. I am holding you close on the rocking chair. You did not do well yesterday and throughout the night. You stopped breathing a few times this morning, and your blue spells are back.

My heart is so broken. But please do not suffer or struggle for our sakes, my love.

I am asking all who follow your story to pray.

Mommy

Friday, October 10, 2008: Update

Dear Darcy,

You are still here but are so weak. I really can't stand to see you struggle and in pain anymore. I know you want to stay because my voice and my heartbeat are all too familiar to you. When I speak, you seem to try harder. When you hear my heartbeat, you take more breaths. I want you to know, honey, that if you leave Mommy, you will be with the Lord. There will be no more suffering, and you will be whole. You will see Mommy again. I have wept, wept, and wept. I love you more than you may ever know, and it is complete torture to see you this way. I am completely amazed at your will to live. I keep thinking, *How much can a tiny body take?*

I can't begin to describe our day. When I see life escape your little body and come back, it tears my heart out. This was my biggest fear of all. To see you suffer. I am just not made for this. At one time, you went ten minutes without breathing. But your heart kept going oh so slowly. You are so close to leaving your mommy's arms. Who am I without you? For the last nine months, my identity has been you. I know you won't make it for much longer. I feel my heart about to burst. What can I do but be by your side when you struggle? As hard as it is to see, how could I leave your side? I must be here, right beside you, to love you and tell you how special you have been to all of us. I wish I could make all of your pain go away. I don't want you to think I want you to go away because I don't. But there is only so much suffering that I can watch you endure. I feel helpless that I cannot do anything to help you.

I always thought the transition from this life to the next was peaceful. Now I wonder why that is not how it is happening. I feel like I must be getting punished, punished for the sin in my life. I feel like I am being tortured. I keep thinking about how much more will happen before I break.

God has been gracious during this enormous trial. Today we celebrated two birthdays for you. The first one, an hour before your actual birthday because we thought you were slipping away. Then when you made it to your actual birthday, we sang again. We gathered with the Smiths and the Brenons and sang hymns. Oh, how peaceful you got when we sang to you. It was a blessing.

It is getting late, and I must get back to your side. I want you to know that even though it hurts and rips my heart out to think about, I am okay for you to go be with Jesus. I know then you will be at real peace and in your glorious body. Please don't stay around for my sake. Part of me dies with you, but all I want now is for you to be healed, full, and at peace. The only place that will happen is in heaven with Jesus. Your two-week journey has been the best two weeks of my life, but they have been full of suffering. It is your time now, your time to be fulfilled and whole. Jesus will be there to greet you. And please know, dear Darcy, by the grace and mercy of our dear Father, I will be there to greet you someday. That day could not come

sooner than I want. But I have all of the faith in
the world that I will see you at that golden gate, to
welcome me to that paradise. And we will worship
the Most High forevermore. I miss you terribly. I
will miss you forever until we see each other face-
to-face again.

I love you, my dear, most blessed child, Darcy.

Mommy

Saturday, October 11, 2008: Day 15

Early this morning, at 2:13, Darcy Anne went
home to be with the Lord forever.

*You keep track of all
my sorrows.*

*You have collected all my
tears in your bottle.*

*You have recorded each
one in your book.*

PSALM 56:8

Darcy, I know that you
are now with your Savior
and are without any pain.
As sad as I am that I will not
see you for a while, I am so
happy that the torment of
this world is no longer on
your shoulders. You were
the most courageous little

girl I have ever known. You moved more people in
your short life than I can even imagine. I love you,
my tiny gift from God. You truly were from the
Lord Most High!

Thank you all for your continued support and
prayers. I have never seen such an outpouring from
people in my entire life. "Thanks" is not enough to
everyone who shared in the excitement of Darcy's
coming and her birth.

I love you, sweet Darcy! I love you! I love you!

Mommy

Saturday, October 11, 2008

Dear Darcy,

We met with the funeral home and received some crushing news. They said that your body is decomposing quickly and there is a high chance that I may not get to see your sweet face again. Or kiss your sweet lips. Or tuck you in. They explained that since you were so small, embalming would probably not be an option and your color would not be conducive to a public viewing. I was holding out hope of seeing you once more. Now we don't know. The coordinator told us that family could view if we wanted to, but since your skin was so thin and transparent, you would probably be significantly darker. I don't want to remember you this way. I want to remember you the way you looked when I held you in my arms. Last night you had a very peaceful look on your beautiful face. You were exactly like you were before all the tubes and wires were taped on your face. You had no imperfections and were perfectly spotless. You had the most beautiful complexion. I will always remember the beauty that shone all around you.

We have set the date for your "heavenly homecoming" for 10:00 a.m. on Thursday, October 16, 2008, at the Klein Funeral Home in Magnolia, Texas.

I miss you terribly already. How do I make it without you? I love you, my sweet gift from God.

Mommy

Sunday, October 12, 2008

Dear Darcy,

Today we all went to church. Being in church was the closest to heaven I could get. I miss you so bad, and I wanted to be close to you. I knew that you were up there praising the Lord, and as we were singing, I imagined that you were singing the same songs in heaven.

Words cannot express how I miss you. I cry every day. I am so happy for you, but I grieve because I miss you terribly. Daddy does too. And your siblings—well, it just isn't the same without you, my sweet child. There are reminders of you every-where. But these *reminders* of you are not *you*. I would love to hold you one last time. Or to touch you. To kiss you. To smell you.

Your daddy and I want to make you proud of us. We have found a renewed commitment and con-nection to each other and to the family. Your life influenced us to put our lives back on the right path. You have moved us to want to do and be better. Thank you for that gift.

I truly believe that you were the best of me. I will never forget the gifts you left behind.

I hope you are having fun up in heaven. You will never be forgotten, my dear child.

I love you, love you, love you.
Mommy

Monday, October 13, 2008

Dear Darcy,

Today Mommy and Daddy went by Daddy's work to pick up his sketch pad and to do some work-related things. Then we picked up pictures of you that we had developed at Sam's Club.

Later in the afternoon, Ms. Anita picked the pictures for the funeral and had them framed. They look awesome! Ms. Shona did an absolutely awesome job.

We stopped to eat at our favorite Thai restaurant and then went by Wal-Mart for a few things. On the way home, we saw a flower shop and stopped and picked out the flowers that we wanted for the funeral. Slowly but surely our funeral arrangements are rolling into motion.

Darcy, I hope that you will like the things that we have planned for you. We are trying to make everything special for you, sweet girl.

I love you, my sweet!
Mommy

Tuesday, October 14, 2008

Dear Darcy,

As I am sitting here thinking about all of the last-minute preparations, I realize that we are so close to saying good-bye, at least for now. I really don't want to. You are everywhere I look. We are preparing your home going as a celebration of your being with Jesus, and I keep thinking, *Why do I feel so alone?* You were a part of me for nine months, and

even as I am helping Daddy prepare for your services, I realize that I am still consumed with you.
And then I think, after Thursday you will be laid
to rest, and then I will no longer have you to tend
to. I will have my memories, but there will be
nothing else that I can do for you. It just makes
me sad.

Our church family continues to do things for
you and your family. It is definitely a labor of
love—from the Stevenses and Smiths, who helped
decorate and prepare for the services, to the elders
and the way they have organized everything. People
say prayers for us, cook meals, help with your
younger siblings, do the errands, and have provided
for every one of our needs. I am overwhelmed and
awed by the power of God at work in His people.
The Lord blesses and continues to bless us.

I love you so much, Darcy. I miss you terribly.
I see myself laugh at your goofy daddy sometimes,
but deep inside I ache for you.

You are my Darcy. I need you.
Mommy

Thursday, October 16, 2008

Dear Darcy,

Today we laid you to rest, my sweet child. It was
the most beautiful service I have ever seen. Thanks
to our loving and supportive church family and
Klein Funeral Home, I could never have imagined
a better homecoming for you. Everyone made it
spectacular, and I mean *spectacular*. You were so

loved, my sweet girl. There was standing room only as people came to see this miracle from God.

We had two miracles today. The first was that I was able to see, kiss, and tuck you in one last time. God preserved your sweet body, and everyone was able to see you as they said their good-byes. This was a miracle, because they were not able to embalm you, and babies of your size do not preserve well. But once again, God in His mercy blessed us with this. God is awesome, as you know now, my sweet baby! Another miracle is that with the 60 to 90 percent chance for rain, we did not see a drop. God graced us again with His presence. People were at your graveside; we had a bagpiper, and it was a very cool afternoon. God rained down His mercy and grace for us again.

We all gave our tributes, and all I can say is that it was awesome. Here was my tribute to you:

> *Dear Darcy,*
>
> *I keep wondering how I can condense sixty-three pages from my blog into just a simple paragraph. I also keep thinking,* How will I be able to speak through so much grief? *But it is the least I can do as a testimony to how God has blessed me through you.*
>
> *What an honor it is to have carried you, given birth to you, and beheld you. I wonder, through all of my sin, why God would bless me in this way, for I am the least deserving. You were the most blessed person that I have ever laid eyes on. Not because of your righteousness but rather by*

how God used you in His mighty way. And I had
the privilege to experience it firsthand. I am all
too familiar with the stories and with how you
impacted so many people. But if the truth be
known, I was in far greater need than anyone of
what God was doing through you. Maybe that is
why He brought you to me.

Darcy, if I could go to heaven right this instant,
I would whisper to you and say, "Thank you.
Thank you for rescuing me from myself." So many
times I catch myself becoming too relaxed in my
faith and not being who God created me to be as
a wife, a mother, and a witness for Christ. But
because of you, I will forever be changed. Your
great sacrifice, though painful and sorrowful, rescued so many for God's sake. And I am at the top
of the list. All I can say is, I love you. I continue
to love you more and more every day.

For the first time, I saw the beauty of God
through someone's eyes, and they were your eyes.
I also saw His beauty in your spirit. I adored your
sweetness. Your beautiful, fighting spirit. And
everything about you. I long to have you back, to
hold you one last time, or to kiss you, or to feel
your soft skin. I know that is not going to happen
on this side of heaven. But one day I will see you
again, and then we will be together forever.

I called you my "Gift from God" because that
is what you were. You were a special gift from
God. Although it is sometimes very hard to
breathe, I am assured that one day I, too, will

*sit with the Most High and be in the company
of special little ones like you. I just miss you so
much. It is so hard for me to imagine life without you on earth. But I am comforted knowing
that you are sitting there with Jesus, especially
knowing the struggles you had on earth. I am so
thankful that your suffering is now over and that
you can live at peace with Jesus. But until we
meet again, I will live with this hole in my heart.
We now have that in common. I love you very
much, my Little Gift from God.*
Mommy

Darcy, I know that you were only the beginning of
this journey. You taught me so much. I know that
I will continue to grieve for you, but I know that
God is with me every step of the way. I love you
and will continue to write to you and let you know
how Mommy is doing. I pray that God in His infi-
nite mercy and grace will heal our broken hearts.

I love you so much!
Mommy

Sunday, October 19, 2008

I knew this was going to be hard, but I didn't know
it would be this hard. I tried preparing myself for
all the possibilities and for telling the kids, but this
is really difficult. When driving alone in the car,
I find myself screaming at the top of my voice, and
I can't stop. It is the deepest, darkest sound that I
have ever heard.

I find myself lashing out at the people who have

hurt me—Lola, for one. She never wanted you to be born and was against Mommy and Daddy having any more children. How could she not want you, especially when so many others were moved by you? God used you in such a mighty way. Lola always loves her grandkids when they are here, but this time was different. You died. How can I forgive this hurt? I know that somehow God will help me, but until then I am trapped with these feelings. How can I feel this anger when you have given me so much? I am not mad with God because He blessed me so much and provided my every desire through this whole journey, but I am finding that I am angry at others. How can I not extend the grace that was so bountifully bestowed on me? Right now I just can't, and I am so ashamed.

In that day the wolf and the lamb will live together; the leopard will lie down with the baby goat. The calf and the yearling will be safe with the lion, and a little child will lead them all.

ISAIAH 11:6

God brought me these two passages from a book that was given to me after your service: "Let the children come to me. Don't stop them! For the Kingdom of God belongs to those who are like these children" (Mark 10:14). And "Beware that you don't look down on any of these little ones. For I tell you that in heaven their angels are always in the presence of my heavenly Father" (Matthew 18:10).

I just can't reason why anyone would have such

disappointment at the news of a baby. And then do and say things that are mean because of it.

Then there are issues with Daddy. It seems as if issues that we have tried to conquer for twenty years are coming to the surface. I guess when something as tragic as losing a child happens, it makes things intensify. Daddy has been under a lot of stress, and he did something that hurt me deeply and that he said he did out of spite during the time when you were so sick and I was caring for you. I can't pretend to know what he is going through, but I don't understand how he could do something so spiteful during a time that I was caring for you, especially knowing what the prognosis was. Again, I lash out at him for hurting me so much and especially during this time. Why did it take your dying for him to finally say that he will stop doing the things that hurt your mommy? I just don't know what to think. For twenty years I made it clear that it hurt me, and that wasn't enough reason for him to stop.

I don't know. Maybe this is all a part of grieving. Maybe I just went over the deep end. I don't know. I just feel my world crumbling, and I shouldn't be feeling this way. I love God. I know He is here for me.

Is this the ugliness of grief? Is this normal? I don't know. But I miss you dearly and know that you would not want Mommy acting or feeling this way. I just don't know my way out. I hope God shows me soon.

I love you, dear Darcy.
Mommy

Sunday, October 19: Update!

Sometimes I wonder at how God works! After a really low day, like when I want to be mad, it seems that God will bring the right person to my rescue at the right time. I don't pretend that this will be an easy road or that all is cured, but I thank God for His people who are really there for me when they say they will be there. Sometimes they say things that I don't want to hear but that are true. Today, I guess I just wanted to be mad at someone and lash out. My husband was that person. I hope the days like today are few, but I pray that when they come, God will send His people to the rescue.

My secret sister and my friend Stacy, from church, came to my aid today after my day of frustration. They gave me the best and most holy advice I could ever hear. In fact, God knew that it was exactly what I needed to hear. Stacy also lost two of her precious children and can truly relate to what I am experiencing. Something she said struck me. She said, "Don't be upset that it took losing Darcy to get Jason to where he is; just be happy he is there." That is very true, even though I didn't want to see it that way earlier. If he is willing to change, then that's what counts. Now I pray that I can see that every day and not dwell on the past, no matter how long we have struggled. I guess it is through pain and suffering that we grow. I am just not seeing clearly while walking through this fresh and difficult road. Stacy also mentioned doing a Tracy List and a list for my other kids, like the one we did for Darcy. I think that is a great idea. Right now, that is the furthest thing from my mind, but I guess it is just baby steps I must take until we reach God's goal for our lives.

My secret sister reminded me of the beautiful atonement that only comes from Christ and that if I accept His atonement for my sins, then I must give forgiveness to others. His atonement is not only for me but also for others. How can I expect His atonement if I can't give that grace to others and forgive them? What a beautiful reminder of where my heart should be. I guess today my mind was just clouded by my own sorrow. My sis also mentioned that she had never seen my face look as dark as it did today. And here I thought I was hiding my grief.

I don't know where all this will lead, but I know that I need to keep writing. If I don't, I feel as if I will lose myself, a little each day. I want to be better for having Darcy. I just thank God for giving me special people to help me in my time of need.

To my secret sister and to Stacy, thank you. You both gave me exactly what I needed today. I love you both.

Tracy

Tuesday, October 21, 2008

Dear Darcy,

Today Mommy took Daddy to work so that he could pick up his motorcycle, which has been in the shop. Daddy loves his motorcycle and has been wanting it back ever since dropping it off. Now he has it back. His motorcycle really reminds him of his ride with you, so it means more now than ever. He is so glad to have it back.

When I came home and when your siblings were done with their schoolwork, we went to visit you. I hope Jesus whispers in your ear when we come to visit you or maybe you are able to look down from heaven and see Mommy there. It makes me feel close to you. I noticed someone came and took your flowers away, so I am going to bring you some the next time I visit.

After our visit with you, we went to Wal-Mart to pick up a present for a birthday party. We went to our former next-door neighbors' house in The Woodlands, because it was their daughter, Julia's, third birthday. It was a great party. You would have loved it. Your siblings really needed a break from all that had happened over the last couple of months. Everyone asked about you and how we were doing. I can tell people are hesitant to ask Mommy about you because they are afraid of upsetting me, but I love talking about you. You are such a big part of my life, and you will always be a part of our family. I don't want to pretend that you didn't exist. Besides, it helps me to talk about you and share what a wonderful baby girl you were to us and others.

At the party, I also got to meet Jack, who was born around the same time you were. I just know that y'all would have been close friends. He is just as cute in person as he was in his pictures. Kata, our other neighbor, is also expecting another baby. I know y'all would have been buddies too. Heaven must be full with an enormous number of friends though, so I know you must be having a blast.

When we came home, we got to see Daddy, who had already made it home from work. We then went and rented the movie *Expelled*, got some ice cream, and watched the movie as a family. We love doing that.

I love you, my precious girl.
Mommy

Thursday, October 23, 2008

Dear Darcy,

I just wanted to post these words of healing, through song, that God is using to help me. God is awesome!

I hope you are having fun in heaven, sweetie! No pain and suffering but mostly being with Jesus, now for eternity!

By Your Side

Why are you striving these days
Why are you looking for love
Why are you still searching as if I'm not enough
To where will you go, child,
Tell me, where will you run
To where will you run
'Cause I'll be by your side
Wherever you fall
In the dead of night

Whenever you call
And please don't fight
These hands that are holding you
My hands are holding you
Look at these hands and my side
They swallowed the grave on that night
When I drank the world's sin
So I could carry you in
And give you life
I want to give you life
'Cause I, I love you
I want you to know
That I, I love you
I'll never let you go

—Tenth Avenue North

Love,
Mommy

Tuesday, October 28, 2008

Dear Darcy,

Mommy misses you so much. I was telling Daddy yesterday that I wish I could just touch you one more time.

We found the culprit behind the flowers missing from your grave. Daddy saw deer hoofprints, and it appears that deer like to eat fresh flowers. So Ate Brittany and I made you a cross of flowers that the deer won't eat. I hope you like them.

Every day is a struggle for your family left on earth. We share all of the sweet memories we had with you, and it makes us sad that we won't have any more. We all love you so much. Little Roman looks at your picture and says, "Darcy!" I just love the way he says your name. Isabella got really sad yesterday, looking at your pictures. Every day there are tears, but most days have been better rather than worse. I guess our worst days are very bad and the better days are coping days. But I am glad our bad days are fewer than our good or "better" days.

Daddy and I visited you yesterday and put up your flowers. You can see them all the way from the parking lot. I really like them. Daddy and I got to talk for a while and just cried, remembering all the things we did with you. It was a really nice talk. One thing about your daddy is that he did everything that Mommy wanted done with you. He wanted to make sure that I had no regrets, and I am not sure there is anyone else who would have done everything I needed. Your daddy is *super*! God must have given him superpowers, because he was able to tend to you and to Mommy. I am so thankful to God for giving us all the wonderful memories we have.

You are so missed, my sweet child. I still get so many cards and e-mails regarding the impact you had on so many people. I am so touched and blessed by all the cards. It is truly amazing. Daddy and Mommy were talking the other night about how most of the cards that are sent to us come from people we don't even know. Most of them! We also get cards and letters from some kids at college. It is absolutely so moving. One lady even mentioned finding out about you from her grandson, who is in college and is praying for you and us. How amazing! I'm ashamed to say that reaching out to people I don't know was the furthest thing from my mind when I was in college. I keep thinking about all the missed blessings because of it. These kids and people have blessed us so much and continue to help us through this difficult time.

Your siblings and Mommy are going to visit you today. I can't wait.

I love you, sweetie.
Mommy

Thursday, October 30, 2008

Dear Darcy,

Yesterday I got to visit a dear friend who had her baby early in the morning. Her baby girl was so precious. I got to hold her, and it reminded me of when I held you just a few short weeks ago, because y'all weighed about the same. It was like holding a piece of heaven. Her name is Elizabeth. She also had trisomy 18 and was not expected to make it to birth. But once again the doctors were wrong. We serve a God bigger than these diseases and bigger than this diagnosis. God blessed this family and allowed them to get to meet their precious little girl and spend time with her before she left for her heavenly home. I am sure that you welcomed her as she came to heaven's door. God blessed you with a friend that is about your age to play with. It is hard to think of not having you and Elizabeth here with us anymore, but I think Daddy

says it right when he says, "Our babies were so spir-
itually gifted that they graduated early to heaven." I
really believe this. Y'all were just so beautiful inside
and out that God wanted you back with Him. And
I praise God that ya'll are with Him, where there is
no suffering and only glory forevermore.

I was listening to this song and wanted to share
these words. God has comforted me so much
through songs this year.

My Tribute

How can I say thanks
For the things You have done for me,
Things so undeserved,
Yet You gave to prove Your love for me.
The voices of a million angels
Could not express my gratitude.
All that I am and ever hope to be,
I owe it all to Thee.

Chorus: *To God be the glory,*
To God be the glory,
To God be the glory,
For the things He has done.
With His blood He has saved me,
With His power He has raised me,
To God be the glory,
For the things He has done.

Just let me live my life,
Let it be pleasing, Lord, to Thee,
And if I gain any praise,
Let it go to Calvary.

With His blood He has saved me,
With His power He has raised me,
To God be the glory,
For the things He has done.

—Andraé Crouch

I love you, Darcy.
Mommy

november

Wednesday, November 12, 2008

Dear sweet Darcy,

Mommy has been really busy with family issues lately but has not forgotten about you. We have been struggling a lot over the last couple of weeks, but God is gracious to see us through, despite our issues. I can't wait to see Him face-to-face, as you do now.

A lot has happened since I last wrote. We got to say good-bye to your sweet little friend Elizabeth, who is right beside you now with Jesus. I imagine y'all holding hands and telling stories about your families here. And now you have the rest of eternity to do it. You know what else, Darcy? God, in all of His mercy, had you and Elizabeth lying beside each other on earth. And having you buried beside each other was all part of God's divine plan. We did not plan it. Gladness overwhelmed me when I saw that she was buried right beside your body. Right beside you! I think of what great friends y'all would have been here, but now you are great friends in heaven. When Mommy and Daddy or your siblings are not there visiting, you will have Elizabeth there.

Bryson has just learned to call out your name instead of just saying, "Baby!" He hears big brother, Roman, say your name, and he always wants to do what big brother does. I love to hear him say your name. Your two big brothers love to see your pictures, and they get such huge smiles on their faces when they see you. I love to see how excited they get when they jump up in my lap to get a closer look at you. We all just love you so very much. And always will. . . .

As we remembered yesterday where we were, just one month ago, we looked at your pictures and videos, and we listened to the music we picked out. We all sat together as a family and remembered all of the wonderful memories that God blessed us with in having you. In spite of all the tears we cried, smiles filled our faces as we also remembered the happiness. Glory be to God for seeing us through to this point.

We approved your headstone today. It should be about six weeks until it's completed. As hard as it is to do things like this, I am just thankful that there are still things that we can do for you. Mommy and Daddy always loved doing things for you. You were and still are such a remarkable little girl. We love you!

I love you, Darcy. We still ache for you. We dream of holding you but will have to wait till God is ready for this ache to be filled. Daddy wrote to you yesterday to say hi and that he loves you.

I will write to you again soon.

Mommy

Wednesday, November 26, 2008

Dear Darcy,

It's been two weeks since I wrote to you. Tomorrow is Thanksgiving Day, and I just wanted to tell you how much I love you and how thankful I am that God gave you to me. It is by far one of my proudest moments to be your mommy. As I have looked back at your pictures, I think how much I cherished you and still do. How can I ever express how blessed I feel to have had you for fifteen days?

I love you.
Mommy

december

Thursday, December 18, 2008

Dear Darcy,

Today is your Meema's birthday. I can only imagine how much fun you must be having as you celebrate with her in heaven. Please give her a hug for me, and tell her how much I love her. I am sure she is sharing so many wonderful stories with you. I love her so much, and I know that she is watching over you until I see you again.

I wanted to share with everyone a letter that was written by one of our elders (on behalf of Darcy) and was read at the funeral. I have wanted to share it for a while but haven't had the time. It is the only letter from Darcy, and it means so much to me. It came about from a dream that my elder had. I see it as a gift from God that expresses the heart of my dear Darcy. Here it is:

> *This letter goes out to all of you who have cried and prayed for me.*
>
> *Let me first say, thanks to all of you for your prayers—I am doing great. Mommy, I know how you worry about me, but there is no need to worry anymore—I have no more pain, no more breathing tube, and my Father is taking incredible care of me. In fact, today Jesus escorted me around the crystal sea. It was so beautiful; I can't wait for*

*all of you to see it with me. For entertainment,
I get to see all of the pictures that were taken of
me over and over and over again. In fact, I had a
contest with some of my friends up here—none of
them had even half of the pictures taken of them.
Thanks to all of you for that gift.*

*To Brittany, Isabella, Alexys, Mallorie, Roman,
and Bryson:*

*I wanted to especially thank each of you for your
love. You were all so kind to me—how you held
me and kissed me and fixed my breathing tube
and cried for me. Bryson, I didn't know it was
you at the time, but I have since discovered that
you kissed me 1,264 times in my few days with
you. Thank you, Brother; they were wonderful
kisses. Brittany, Bella, and Alexys, you treated me
with great gentleness—just like Mommy. Thank
you for that—you guys will make great mommies
one day. I just know that you would have been the
best brothers and sisters to grow up with. While I
wish it was longer, I have thanked my Father for
the time He gave me with each of you.*

Dear Mommy and Daddy,

*I understand now why you were crying for me.
And because of that, I have cried for you, too.
But don't worry, Mommy; don't worry, Daddy;
my Father is wiping all of my tears away; and He
promised me that He would do the same for you.*
I didn't understand what trisomy 18 was, and

while I still don't fully understand it, I thank you for allowing us to meet and spend so much time together. I have met many other people in heaven who had trisomy 18. Few of them were allowed to be born; and even fewer yet were able to spend time snuggling with their parents like I did with you guys. I know you had the choice to not let me be born. I know you had the choice to not revive me those three times the other night. And while you thought I was in pain, it was nothing compared to the inexpressible joy of being able to spend a few more days with you. Thank you for choosing life.

Mommy and Daddy, I have been told that I affected many people and even saved some people's lives. I don't fully understand all of this, but I know that you had a lot to do with that. I have a large room in my Father's house, but I have seen the room our Father is preparing for you, and it has recently been filled with many more treasures.

To my daddy:

Some told you that I was "incompatible with life"—thank you for not believing that. You worked so hard to give me a full life while I was there with you. I could not believe all the things you planned for me and all the things I was able to do with the family. The checklist of activities you made for me is etched forever in my mind. I really liked the motorcycle ride, but my favorite part was our Daddy-daughter dance. Daddy,

I realized after I got here that it was your strength that helped me to live so long. You put something in me that made me refuse to quit; but when my Father called me home, well . . . even your strength, Daddy, can't compare.

Mommy,

I know that you will be most upset this day, and there is little I can do to change that. I want you to know that I have read every letter you wrote to me, and I understand that you weep because of your love for me. Mommy, please know: I love you, too. I was with you just a few days it seems, but we really bonded. You are forever my mommy, but you are also the closest friend I had—I will never forget our time on the swing together. You stared at me, you held me, you seemed to never sleep while I was with you. When you spoke, I was awakened with hope; when you sang to me, I was comforted. For two full weeks—no, for nine months and two full weeks—you poured your life into me . . . and you knew I wasn't going to live! Mommy, that sacrificial love is similar to what Jesus did for us. Thank you, Mommy; oh, thank you for your love.

It is time for me to close this letter now. I want to let all of you know, Mommy and Daddy, broth-ers and sisters, friends and family, you worked so hard to give me a life of happiness, to make me comfortable, and to make me feel at home. But where you are . . . is not my home. You celebrated

every moment of my life, Mommy and Daddy,
but now I am really living! Now, I am truly
home!
Until we see each other again . . .
Love and hugs and kisses,

Darcy Anne Ramos,
one of whom the world was not worthy

Thank You, God, for laying on the heart of my
elder and friend these words that relieve my suffering and let me know the thoughts and desires of
my precious child.

I love you, sweet Darcy.
Mommy

Friday, December 19, 2008

Dear Darcy,

Daddy and Mommy have been reflecting on this
past year, and we feel truly humbled and blessed
by the graciousness of God and what He has done
for us. So many people have come to our aid and
have blessed us because of you. God brought many
people into our lives to be testimonies of the one
true living God! You truly were a living testimony
that has left an imprint and continues to leave an
imprint on the hearts of many. I bet when you see
the face of Jesus, you can see all of His majesty and
wonder. You can see how He works through your
life, even though you have now gone to be with
Him. Are you as amazed as we are down here? He
really is as awesome as we see, isn't He? We see

Him through faith; you see Him through sight. What an awesome thought!

Darcy, Mommy is so happy for you! I miss you so much but can only imagine the splendor that you are experiencing now. We are about to celebrate our Savior's birth, and I know that His birthday party in heaven is far greater than the ones we had for you here. I hope you have a great time at Jesus' birthday party and know that Mommy, Daddy, Brittany, Isabella, Alexys, Mallorie, Roman, and Bryson are celebrating with you. Praise Him, praise Him!

I love you, my dearest, sweet baby!
Mommy

I will thank you, Lord, among all the people. I will sing your praises among the nations. For your unfailing love is as high as the heavens. Your faithfulness reaches to the clouds. Be exalted, O God, above the highest heavens. May your glory shine over all the earth.

PSALM 57:9-11

Wednesday, December 24, 2008

Dear Darcy,

What a wonderful day we had. We all are excited and are surrounded with love and support from our friends. We went by and visited you. When we got there, we noticed that you had received a Christmas gift—you got your headstone! It looks really good!

We went through the day and watched as your siblings got so excited about all the gifts. Finally the time came to open them. We were so blessed by the people from Project

Hope who bring gifts to families who have lost children. I was so moved by what someone said. She said, "Thank you for making my Christmas better!" It was very emotional for Mommy and Daddy to see another way we were blessed by God because of you! We cried and cried! We miss you so much!

I imagine you preparing a *big* birthday party for Jesus. I hope you have a lot of fun at His party.

I love you, sweetie!
Mommy

Thursday, December 25, 2008

Happy birthday, Jesus!

Please tell my little Darcy hello for me! We miss her so much, and especially during this time of celebrating the day You were born. But we get sad because we want to celebrate with her in body but must do so in spirit. Please, Lord, comfort us with Your all-sufficient grace and mercy.

Dear Darcy,

We spent the day reminiscing about Jesus and preparing dinner because we had some special friends from church coming by. When they got here, we had some wonderful food and fellowship. I showed off the new throw that Ate Brittany got for me. It was the picture of me kissing you. It is so beautiful. We also all received sweatshirts with your signature picture on it and pillowcases with your picture, and I got a purse with your picture on it. I guess everyone knew that gifts that reminded me of you would make me feel happy. I will always cherish the gifts that were given on your behalf from the precious people at Project Hope. *Thank you!* These gifts are constant reminders of the precious time our Lord and Savior gave us with you. God is so good! We have been enormously blessed this year. Thank You, Lord Jesus, for all of Your wonderful gifts—You being the number one gift!

I love you, Darcy, sweet child. I look forward to seeing you again someday in heaven!

Mommy

Friday, December 26, 2008

Dear Darcy,

Today we went and visited you! We brought you some gifts and a card. I hope you like them. We love you and miss you so much.

Today I listened to a song by MercyMe that I've heard a thousand times. It just rings true to how I feel. I love the bridge where it talks about laying a tiny offering at God's feet. It reminds me of giving you as a tiny offering and laying you at the feet of Jesus. And it really is a small sacrifice compared to the one at Calvary.

Here are the lyrics:

God with Us

Who are we
That you would be mindful of us
What do you see
That's worth looking our way

We are free
In ways that we never should be
Sweet release
From the grip of these chains.
Like hinges straining from the weight
My heart no longer can keep from singing

Chorus: *All that is within me cries*
For you alone be glorified
Emmanuel
God with us
My heart sings a brand new song
The debt is paid these chains are gone
Emmanuel
God with us

Lord you know
Our hearts don't deserve your glory
Still you show
A love we cannot afford
Like hinges straining from the weight
My heart no longer can keep from singing

[bridge]
Such a tiny offering compared to Calvary
Nevertheless we lay [her] at your feet

This song really brings to life the reality of this truth. Anything that we give up on this earth, no matter how big or small, is really a tiny offering compared to what God has done on Calvary.

I love you, Darcy.
Mommy

Tuesday, January 6, 2009

Dear Darcy,

I remember where I was just a year ago, when God had not yet woven you together in my womb. I could not fathom how I could survive and go through life if I had known back then that I was going to lose you. But God in His mercy and grace carried me through it all. In fact, He didn't just carry me through it—I am better because of it. So many other people are too. I am better from just knowing you, Darcy. I always said that I could never endure losing one of my children, and yet here I am. I really miss you, Darcy. But God has conquered death and the grave, and that is what brings me comfort every day. Knowing that He rescued you, I know that He will someday rescue me, too. There will, indeed, be a day in which we will never be separated again.

I love you, love you, love you . . . and miss you terribly.

Mommy

Tuesday, January 13, 2009

Dear Darcy,

It's been a week since I last wrote, and Mommy misses you so much! Things have been very exciting around here, but I can't tell you much until everything works itself out. Just know that Mommy and Daddy love and miss you so much.

One thing I can tell you is that a friend of mine wrote to me today and asked to share your story. Her husband is speaking for Blogs 4 Life, located at the Family Research Council in Washington, D.C. It is also going to be broadcast, and I am so excited that God is still using you and sharing your miraculous journey. Like you, my friend's baby boy was born with a medical condition, and they were advised to abort. Instead, they decided to keep their son. You should see how big and beautiful he is now.

God is so great! I can't believe how He continues to show Himself in such mighty ways. If more people, Darcy, came to know Christ through your story, it would be awesome. God is still choosing to use you. I am just so unworthy to have a front-row seat.

Grandpa is coming to visit next week. I can't wait for him to see all the beautiful pictures of you. Your siblings are so excited to see him. He likes to play games and is a lot of fun. Grandpa also is the one God used to teach Mommy about Him. You see, Darcy, sometimes God uses people in life and in death to bring glory to Himself. What an awesome God He is!

I love you, sweetheart. I hope you can feel it! Mommy is waiting for the day when I can see your face again.

Mommy

Friday, January 23, 2009

Dearest Darcy,

The time has come to close this part of your bitter-sweet journey and to close your journal. I didn't realize it would be this difficult. I can barely see through all of my tears, and I can hardly breathe. But it is what God requires of me now, and I must willingly surrender.

The reason I must close your Web site is that God led people at Tyndale House Publishers to make a book about your life. With that comes closing your journal. I believe that God chose you for such a time as this, even as He is choosing me now. This book will be written so that others may experience the power and grace of our loving Father in the story of what He's done through you. Your life is a powerful testimony of how precious every life is from the moment of conception. You see, sweet Darcy, God wants to use you for His service, and you are His, not mine. Your life, your story, and your testimony belong to Him, and I can no longer hold on to something that wasn't mine to begin with. I have held on to your diary as a way to hold on to that small part of you that I have left. It has been my way of knowing that you were once with me and that your legacy will live on. Now, without my journal, your death suddenly seems so real.

God is going to reach so many others with the message that we must start valuing and protecting human life. Your story has saved lives, and with the next phase, through your book, many more will not only live but live abundantly, like you did. I have been forever changed by knowing you. Even though I must end this part of the journey, please know that your death will not be in vain. By God's grace, I will carry your torch to help in the fight for precious life. Everyone deserves a chance to live, especially those who do not have voices of their own. You lived a good life. Every precious baby deserves a chance.

Darcy, when I think of the past year, I never cease to be amazed at how good God is. My faith in Him has grown because of you. How couldn't it when His miracles were so real? There are numerous undeniable proofs of how God worked through you. I hope to elaborate more on all of the ways God showed Himself to us through miracles. We have never felt as humbled as we have in the past year. I do not believe that anything happened by coincidence. Everything is a part of God's divine plan. God gave us these reminders to strengthen our faith and reliance on Him and to fortify your family's bond. We will never be the same.

Thank you, Darcy, for being a part of our lives. We will remember to honor your memory and to please God in doing so. Romans 8:28 states, "We know that God causes everything to work together for the good of those who love God and are called according to his purpose for them."

Before I end, I heard another song today that just jumped into my soul. It is "Cannons" by Phil Wickham:

It's falling from the clouds
A strange and lovely sound
I hear it in the thunder and the rain.
It's ringing in the skies
Like cannons in the night
The music of the universe plays.
Singing, You are holy, great and mighty
The moon and the stars declare who You are.
I'm so unworthy, but still You love me
Forever my heart will sing of how great You are
Beautiful and free
The song of galaxies
Reaching far beyond the Milky Way
Let's join in with the sound
Come on let's sing it out
As the music of the universe plays
All glory, honor, power is Yours, Amen.
All glory, honor, power is Yours, Amen.
All glory, honor, power is Yours, forever Amen.

Know this, Darcy. You will live on in the hearts and minds of people forever. You will change lives. You will save lives. I'm looking forward to witnessing all that will be made plain.

I look forward to seeing you again someday. I will miss you terribly until then. I love you, I love you, I love you, my sweet child.

Mommy

Postscript

Although life at the Ramoses is starting to resemble a somewhat routine pace, life after Darcy has felt as if we are suspended in another reality. Darcy shook our complacency by causing us to reevaluate many of the ways we viewed circumstances and treated people. She compelled us to rely fully on God and to trust in His providence.

It's true that we experienced new depths of pain and anguish, but as is the case with any life-changing experience, we are forever changed because Darcy accomplished the purpose God had for her coming. Little Darcy led us to love more deeply, to forgive, to have faith, to never limit God's power, to accept His grace and pass it on, to seek more closeness with God, and to abandon our sinful pasts and move ahead to new beginnings.

Our children Brittany, Isabella, Alexys, Mallorie, Roman, and Bryson learned that living the abundant life is about making the right choices and that the choices they make have temporal and eternal consequences.

God sent Darcy to us to help us heal. This is our new normal.

As for the thousands of family members, friends, and caring strangers from all over the world who visited the Web site, Darcy's impact on them was

profound too. Perhaps the greatest change occurred
in the hearts of those who, before reading about
Darcy, had already made the choice (and had even
set up appointments) to have abortions but later
changed their plans. Many have renewed their rela-
tionships, not just with the Lord but with their
loved ones, especially their children.

> *In that day the wolf and the lamb will live
> together; the leopard will lie down with the
> baby goat. The calf and the yearling will be
> safe with the lion, and a little child will lead
> them all.*
>
> ISAIAH 11:6

About the Author

Tracy Frisbie Ramos is the mother and home educator of six living children, ages two to eighteen. She was born and raised in Fort Worth, Texas. She and her husband, Jason, met and married at Bennigan's Restaurant in Arlington, Texas, in 1989. They currently live in Magnolia, Texas.

Tracy's mission in life is to serve the Lord by raising godly children who will make a difference for His Kingdom on earth. It is Tracy's hope that the legacy of her seventh child, Darcy Anne, will continue to spread the message that children are a gift from God and that the life of the unborn is sacred and should be protected.

For more information about any of the ministry organizations listed in *Letters to Darcy*, please visit the sites listed below.

Heavenly Angels in Need
41300 Upper Calapooia Dr.
Sweet Home, OR 97386
www.heavenlyangelsinneed.com

Now I Lay Me Down to Sleep (NILMDTS)
7201 S. Broadway Suite 150
Littleton, CO 80122
www.nowilaymedowntosleep.org

tracy ramos

Garden of Innocence
www.gardenofinnocence.org

String of Pearls
www.stringofpearlsonline.com